THE POSITIVE
SCHOOL OF
CRIMINOLOGY

ENRICO FERRI

THE POSITIVE
SCHOOL OF
CRIMINOLOGY
THREE LECTURES
BY ENRICO ⌐FERRI

EDITED, WITH AN INTRODUCTION
BY STANLEY E. GRUPP

BIOGRAPHICAL ESSAY
BY THORSTEN SELLIN

UNIVERSITY OF PITTSBURGH PRESS

PREFACE

ENRICO Ferri's three lectures given at the University of Naples in 1901 represent both a defense of the Positive School and a presentation of its basic tenets, as well as a reasoned attack on the Classical School of Criminology. It should be remembered that in their written and translated form the lectures must inevitably lose something of their original quality. One such partial loss is Enrico Ferri's colorful oratorical skill. But even this feature of Ferri's person is to some extent evident in the present volume. To the reader unfamiliar with Ferri's work it will soon be apparent why he was known as a fiery orator and why Jerome Hall has referred to Ferri as having a "volatile imagination."[1]

To assist the new reader and reacquaint others with Ferri, comments in the Introduction have been confined to selected

1. Jerome Hall, *Principles of Criminal Law* (Indianapolis: Bobbs-Merrill, 1947), 548.

issues raised in, or suggested by, the lectures themselves. The intent of the Introduction is to speak of these issues and not to review all aspects of the life and work of Enrico Ferri.

Some of the names and references in the lectures may not be known to English readers. As often as possible (as determined by the availability of information) brief informational footnotes have been provided the first time unfamiliar names are used. Typically, however, detailed information regarding proper names is not needed to understand the context.

Footnotes are numbered separately for the Introduction, for Professor Sellin's biographical review and assessment of the life and work of Enrico Ferri, and for each of Ferri's lectures.

The content of the three lectures is taken from the 1913 imprint of the Ernest Untermann translation, entitled *The Positive School of Criminology*, copyrighted and published in 1906 by Charles H. Kerr and Company of Chicago. The changes that have been made are those instances where spellings were wrong, where there were errors in proper names, and where miscellaneous errors could be corrected beyond reasonable doubt. With the exception of certain obvious misprints which have been silently corrected, changes are indicated by brackets in the text or are cited in footnotes. Minor changes have also been made in punctuation, mainly in the way of modernizing it where it seemed desirable to do so for the reader's benefit. Titles have also been added to each of the lectures, in order to identify the subject of the lecture.

Special thanks are due Professor Thorsten Sellin for permission to reprint his perceptive statement on Enrico Ferri, which originally appeared in the Pioneers in Criminology series published in *The Journal of Criminal Law, Criminology and Police Science*. I wish also to express my appreciation to Dr. Robert G. Caldwell for his helpful comments on a draft of the Introduction, to my colleague Dr. Robert Sutherland for his illuminating syntactical insights, and to Mrs. Alberta Carr for her inimitable skill in typing and proofreading the manuscript.

S.E.G.

CONTENTS

THE POSITIVE
SCHOOL OF
CRIMINOLOGY

INTRODUCTION

STANLEY E. GRUPP

Too often the progenitors in any given field are all but neglected with the course of time. This situation certainly holds true for criminology, and for Enrico Ferri—the most vociferous spokesman, defender, and proselytizer of the Positive School of Criminology in the late nineteenth and early twentieth centuries. The three lectures printed here capture the driving force of criminological positivism, as well as the spirit which drove Ferri to argue endlessly for the scientific study of man and to extol the benefits he felt would result from this study. Equally important is his vitriolic attack on the "juridical abstractions" of the Classical School of Criminology.

It has now been nearly forty years since Enrico Ferri's death and a half century since the publication by Little, Brown and Company of the fourth edition of *Criminal Sociology*, his work best known to the English-speaking world. *The Positive School of Criminology* is a lesser-known work comprising three lectures given by Ferri at the University of Naples, Italy, in April 1901. This volume was originally published in an apparently limited edition in 1906 by Charles H. Kerr and Company of Chicago, primarily a socialist publishing house. The value of these lectures will soon be apparent to those reading them for the first time. Those rereading them will be reminded anew of the spirit, drive, and faith of this early proponent of scientific criminology; they will see too a kind of commitment seldom found today. Those not acquainted with Professor Thorsten Sellin's excellent discussion of the life and work of Ferri will find it of inestimable value in gaining an understanding of him.

Ferri was no ordinary person, for without him it is possible that developments in criminology, especially in the United States, would have taken a considerably different path. While some may wish these developments had been otherwise, it cannot be denied that the placing of the traditional criminology course in sociology departments is due in part to Ferri's coined phrase, "criminal sociology."[1] But Ferri's impact extends beyond this, for it was the Positive School of Criminology as it emerged in late nineteenth century Italy which set the stage and provided the impetus for the growth of scientific criminology. In recognition of this contribution, which is in large part Ferri's, Leon Radzinowicz has said, "Virtually every element of value in contemporary criminological knowledge owes its formulation to that very remarkable school of Italian criminologists. . . ."[2]

It should be noted, however, that there is considerable disagreement in the literature about the impact and importance of the Positive School as it emerged under the influence of Ferri and Lombroso.[3] Although the emphasis on the biological, psychological, and social dimensions of criminological investigation

1. See Gilbert Geis, "Sociology, Criminology, and Criminal Law," *Social Problems*, Vol. 7, Summer 1959, 40–47.
2. Leon Radzinowicz, *In Search of Criminology* (London: Heinemann Educational Books, 1961), p. 3. Ch. 1, "Pioneer and Dogma," discusses Italian criminology in its historical and present-day context.
3. See, for example, Alfred Lindesmith and Yale Levin, "The Lombrosian

has varied through the years, its central focus on the scientific study of the criminal himself is derived directly from the Ferri–Lombrosian tradition. The loose, somewhat eclectic framework which emerged has dominated criminology in the United States throughout the first half of the twentieth century.

The Positive School of Criminology is generally recognized as having its origin in late nineteenth century Italy. Lindesmith and Levin have considered this recognition to be based on a "myth,"[4] but there was no doubt in Ferri's mind about where the credit belonged. Although he was well acquainted with the work of early nineteenth century social scientists such as Quetelet and Guerry, Ferri makes it eminently clear in the opening words of his first lecture that the "new science" of criminology was "born" in Italy. While both the "birth" of criminology as a science and the contributions of the late nineteenth century Italians may be open to debate, the impetus their work gave to scientific criminology, whatever its merits, can hardly be questioned. Of perhaps greater importance, however, are Ferri's ferocious attack on the Classical School and his defense of the rehabilitative ideal, both an integral part of the Positive School.

The scope of the Ferri–Lombrosian tradition is much broader than the stereotype of biological determinism commonly assigned to them would indicate. As Mannheim has stated, "The theoretical system of the positivists is far more comprehensive than their specifically anthropological–biological doctrines, and . . . positivists can be found among criminologists who do not

Myth in Criminology," *The American Journal of Sociology*, Vol. 42, Mar. 1937, 653–71, and Thorsten Sellin's reply, "Letter to the Editor," Vol. 42, May 1937, 897–99. See also Hermann Mannheim's discussion in *Pioneers in Criminology*, ed. Hermann Mannheim, (Chicago: Quadrangle Books, 1960), Ch. 1. More recently David Matza has attacked the "hard" determinism of the Positive School. See David Matza, *Delinquency and Drift* (New York: John Wiley and Sons, 1964), esp. Ch .1.

4. Lindesmith and Levin, "The Lombrosian Myth in Criminology. Wolfgang has labeled the Lindesmith–Levin article as an "unwarranted denouncement of Lombroso." See Marvin E. Wolfgang, "Pioneers in Criminology: Cesare Lombroso (1835–1909)," *The Journal of Criminal Law, Criminology and Police Science*, Vol. 52, Nov.–Dec. 1961, 384.

3

support these doctrines."[5] Ferri, guided by his commitment to the scientific study of the offender, sought the explanation for criminal behavior in areas beyond the biological dimension. The philosophical foundations underlying his approach also served to support his position with respect to the objective of punishment, namely, rehabilitation.

The belief that some persons were biologically predestined to a life of crime was an integral part of much criminological thinking in the late nineteenth and early twentieth century. Ferri himself supported this view. It is nevertheless to Ferri's enduring credit that in considering the cause of criminal behavior at a time when biological determinism was at its prime, he recognized the need to consider the biological dimension in its interrelationship with psychological, social, and telluric factors. Today, the prepotency of the biological factor is all but rejected in the United States, where research and teaching have been primarily in the hands of social environmentalists.[6]

Ferri's support of the view that crime rates among certain ethnic groups can be explained by their "racial character" and "blood" (Lecture III) receives little, if any, acceptance today. Again, however, it seems unfair to condemn him for this attitude. Considering the intellectual climate of the time in which he wrote and lived—it was the heyday of biological Darwinism—it is all the more striking that Ferri minimized the biological factor as much as he did.

Ferri's assumption that crime must be studied in the offender has been severely criticized. Jeffery, among others, has emphasized that a distinction must be drawn between "crime" and "criminal behavior." He states, ."The term 'crime' refers to the act of judging or labeling the behavior, rather than to the behavior itself. Why people behave as they do and why the

5. Hermann Mannheim, *Comparative Criminology* (Boston: Houghton Mifflin, 1965), p. 222.
6. But see Eckland's plea for an integration of genetic and sociological principles. Bruce K. Eckland, "Genetics and Sociology: A Reconsideration," *American Sociological Review*, Vol. 32, Apr. 1967, 173–94.

behavior is regarded as criminal are two separate problems requiring different types of explanations."[7] The importance of observations of this kind notwithstanding, the major concern for American criminologists has been that which Ferri advocated —the individual criminal. Cautions in a similar vein, calling attention to the problems which emerge when the subject matter of criminology is divorced from the criminal law, have been voiced by Francis Allen, Robert G. Caldwell, Jerome Hall, Paul Tappan, and others.

In these three short lectures Ferri touches on a wide array of subjects. The pivotal points are his sustained attack upon the Classical School of Criminology and his persistence in placing criminology and the framework for dealing with the criminal on a scientific footing. Each lecture, however, has a different focus. The first is a frontal assault on the Classical School. Causes of criminality and Ferri's classification of criminals are stressed in the second. In the third, attention is directed to the remedies and program proposed by the Positive School. Most of Ferri's ideas are only briefly explored in the lectures.[8] This is especially true of many of the issues considered in Lectures II and III. Thus, it should be emphasized that the value of the three lectures does not lie in their detailed description of the extensive nuances of the Positive School of Criminology—since only their bare outlines are set forth—but in the fact that in a few words the driving spirit and the dedicated commitment of the Positive School are clearly captured.

The Positive School shares with the Classical School of a century earlier a commitment to reform in the handling of the criminal. Beyond this, however, there is little agreement between the two schools, primarily because they each make different assumptions about the nature of man and the function

7. Clarence Ray Jeffery, "The Historical Development of Criminology," *The Journal of Criminal Law, Criminology and Police Science*, Vol. 50, June 1959, 6.

8. In addition to reading Professor Sellin's scholarly statement, the interested reader should consult Enrico Ferri, *Criminal Sociology* (Boston: Little, Brown, 1917).

of punishment. These differences between the Classical and Positive Schools, and the innumerable problems emanating from them, remain very high on the list of issues, still unresolved, to which Ferri addressed himself.

In sum, the Classical School believed that the greatest happiness of the greatest number was the primary objective of punishment, and saw deterrence as the means of achieving this condition. Underlying and partly sustaining these objectives was the assumption that man is a rational, calculating creature who weighs the consequences of his projected behavior before acting. Paralleling this concept was a reaction against the extreme capriciousness and too-often barbarous nature of punishment in the eighteenth century. To deal with these issues and to achieve its stated objectives, the Classical School proposed the establishment of a scale of penalties which would reflect the gravity of the crime. It was felt that such a plan would insure maximum protection to society and the individual.

While Ferri recognized the contribution made by the Classical School at the time of its inception, particularly with respect to the mitigation of penalties, he felt that it had long since outlived its usefulness. The Classical School was a "mere reform . . . a small step forward" compared to the Positive School, which Ferri saw as directing itself to "a complete and fundamental transformation of criminal justice itself . . ." (Lecture I). It is apparent that Ferri's argument is inextricably interwoven with a deep faith in science as the best means of solving man's problems. As Matza has said, "The strange thing about hard determinism is its extreme gullibility. It is a 'scientific' philosophy imbued with faith and given to utopian promise."[9] But Ferri, like many persons with a cause, did not recognize the limits of the position he defended. In his attack upon the Classical School and his parallel defense of the scientific study of man, he failed to recognize that he was substituting one dogma for another. Certainly Ferri was not sensitized to the admonishing question

9. Matza, *Delinquency and Drift*, note 3 on pp. 93–94.

posed by Professor Jerome Hall, who asks what determines the determinism of the determinist.[10] With his challenge to the Classical School, Ferri contributed to the creation of the free will–determinism dichotomy which continues to harass us and which still presents a dilemma in deciding how to view the adjudicated criminal and what to do with him. This is perhaps the most difficult of the issues to which Ferri addressed himself. But for Ferri, there was no doubt—since the world was a determined entity—that science was *the* answer to man's problems.

In the name of science and therefore in the best interests of society, Ferri did allow for the complete indeterminate incarceration of some individuals. In contrast, the Classical School, rejected by Ferri, placed definite limits on what the representatives of the state could do to the adjudicated criminal. Under the system envisioned by Ferri, however, it was assumed that scientists would not abuse the power which would in fact be theirs. It is clear then, that Ferri did not make a distinction between science as a method and science as an end.

Although Ferri supported the indeterminate sentence and saw it as an administrative procedure, he also seemed to have realized the need for some restraints on complete indeterminate segregation. In the third lecture he indicates the need for "organs of guardianship" for such persons and the need for "permanent committees for the periodical revision of sentences." Presumably, however, such committees would be manned by the experts themselves, and would not serve as a check on their power.

It was Ferri's conviction that the Classical School placed too much emphasis on the retributive–repressive function of punishment. Indeed, he seems to equate punishment with retribution. According to Ferri, it would be possible, under the guiding hand of the Positive School, to relegate repressive measures to an "unimportant role." He argues that since retributive measures are applied after the fact, they do not prevent criminal behavior. "It is a remedy directed against effects but it does not

10. Jerome Hall, *Principles of Criminal Law* (Indianapolis: Bobbs–Merrill, 1947), p. 529.

touch the causes, the roots, of the evil" (Lecture III). Historical rhetoric notwithstanding, and regardless of one's position with respect to the objectives of punishment, most would today agree with Jerome Hall when he states, "It is now recognized that the 'prevention of crime' and the 'protection of society' are ends accepted by everyone, and that the reiteration of such slogans does not solve problems."[11]

Today the Positive School has been attacked for its "hard" determinism and those identified with the school not uncommonly serve as straw men for those whose antipathies are aroused by the thought of biological determinism. Interestingly, however, some of the School's critics, like Ferri himself, place an inordinate emphasis upon the rehabilitative function of punishment—to the virtual neglect of the deterrent and retributive objectives. Thus the problems posed by the potential tyranny of the expert remain as ominous today as ever. The heart of the matter is clearly identified by Professor Francis Allen:

> The obligation of containing power within the limits suggested by a community's political values has been considerably complicated by the rise of the rehabilitative ideal. For the problem today is one of regulating the exercise of power by men of good will, whose motivations are to help not to injure, and whose ambitions are quite different from those of the political observer so familiar to history.[12]

Similarly, it is the prevailing rehabilitative function of punishment, in part supported and sustained by scientific ideology and intermixed with an impersonal and variegated humanitarianism, which prompted Samuel Fahr to observe that, given the limitations of our knowledge, we have assumed too much. The reformation–individualization approach "is invoked in the name

11. Jerome Hall, *General Principles of Criminal Law* (Indianapolis: Bobbs-Merrill, 1960), pp. 307–08.
12. Francis A. Allen, "Criminal Justice, Legal Values and the Rehabilitative Ideal," *The Journal of Criminal Law, Criminology and Police Science,* Vol. 50, Sept.–Oct. 1959, 230. See also the references cited in note 14.

of kindness, but it can have its cruel side . . . [and] this aspect of humanitarianism turned upside down is not only implicit, it rises to the dignity of explicit assertion."[13]

Ferri, convinced that punishment does not deter and that retribution must be kept to the minimum, maintained that the rehabilitative function of punishment should be *the* guiding principle in the prevention of criminal behavior and in the handling of the criminal. In his eagerness to emphasize his point, however, he sometimes stacks the evidence. Early in Lecture II, for example, he suggests that Jeremy Bentham recognized the inefficacy of punishment as a deterrent. Bentham's true stand—basic support of the deterrent theory—was, of course, well known to Ferri. The same may not have been true for some students in Ferri's audience.

Since Ferri's era there has been an ascendancy of the rehabilitative theory of punishment. This trend notwithstanding, some persons, myself among them, would include the deterrent and retributive functions of punishment as legitimate objectives to be sought.[14] The issue is extremely complex. The search for a single rationale for punishment is surely as hopeless as the search for a single cause of criminal behavior.[15] Given the assumption that punishment serves multiple objectives, more difficult and complex questions emerge than Ferri's punitive–rehabilitative dichotomy suggests: Who will be affected, and under what circumstances? What will be the total effect of dealing with a given individual in a particular way?

The ascendancy of the rehabilitative ideal during the twen-

13. Samuel Fahr, "Why Lawyers Are Dissatisfied With the Social Sciences," *Washburn Law Journal,* Vol. 1, Spring 1961, 164.

14. Robert G. Caldwell has been one of the more articulate spokesmen for this point of view. See Robert G. Caldwell, *Criminology* (New York: The Ronald Press, 1965), Ch. 17, and his review of the third edition of the American Correctional Association's *Manual of Correctional Standards, 1966,* appearing in the *American Journal of Correction,* Vol. 28, Nov.–Dec. 1966, 4–6. See also Hall, *General Principles of Criminal Law,* note 11, Ch. 9.

15. Leon Radzinowicz, *Ideology and Crime* (New York: Columbia University Press, 1966), Ch. 4.

tieth century is within the Ferri tradition. It is evident, however, that we have not reached the state envisioned by Ferri, in which scientists decide what should be done with the criminal. It may be said that although concern about crime and the criminal seems to have gained momentum during the seventh decade of the twentieth century, we do not have anything approaching an agreement on what specifically can or should be done.[16] Similarly, both professionals and laymen often disagree about when a particular procedure should be applied and how it should be implemented. These several factors should be kept in mind in any discussion of the acceptance or rejection of points of view regarding crime, criminals, penal practices, and procedures, be they ideas associated with Ferri or with others.

Among Ferri's ideas which have gained wide acceptance today are many of the "preventive–social hygiene" measures or "substitutes for punishment" he supported. In his third lecture, Ferri conceived of "two widely different kinds of repression," police prevention and social prevention. His almost exclusive emphasis was, of course, on social prevention, for "social remedies must be applied to social ills." Envisioned by Ferri were a host of techniques and procedures designed to strike at the causes of criminality. After citing a number of these, Ferri stops short, saying, "I might stray pretty far, if I were to continue these illustrations of social hygiene which will be the true solution of the problem and the supreme systematic, daily humane, and bloodless remedy against the disease of criminality" (Lecture III). Here is clear evidence of Ferri's commitment to broad-sweeping social reforms in order to deal with the problem of criminality.[17] We would find Ferri much in agreement with the "great society" and "lighted streets" approach of today. In a similar vein is his concept of compensating the

16. Witness, for example, the Report by the President's Commission on Law Enforcement and Administration of Justice, *The Challenge of Crime in a Free Society* (Washington, D. C.: United States Government Printing Office, 1967).

17. Ferri's recommended social reforms for dealing with the criminal problem were much akin to his political views. He supported those po-

victims of crime. While not an original contribution of Ferri, this approach was nevertheless supported by him. Renewed interest in the subject today makes this fact worth noting.[18]

Had it not been for Enrico Ferri, criminology—whatever its strengths and weaknesses—would not be the same today. Much of the credit for the influence of the Positive School of Criminology in stimulating the scientific study of the criminal goes to Enrico Ferri, the leading spokesman for the School. Similarly, were it not for Ferri, we would be less able to reflect intelligently on the function of punishment, be it deterrence, rehabilitation, retribution, or a combination of these.

The value of *The Positive School of Criminology* is well expressed by the words of Edward Shils with reference to classical works in sociology:

A classic is not a monument. It is a continuous opportunity for contact with an enduring problem, with a permanently important aspect of existence, as disclosed through the greatness of a mind. It never becomes archaic, even if its stylistic idiom is out of fashion. It remains a classic as long as the problems with which it deals remain problematic, relevant, and insoluble in any definitive way. It becomes a monument of a great human achievement once the problem ceases to be relevant to contemporary concerns, or when its solution is permanently transcended by a better solution.[19]

---

litical ideologies which seemed to have the greatest potential for realizing the objectives of the Positive School of Criminology. In this connection (as discussed by Sellin), during the course of his life Ferri moved from strong socialist attachments to a position of similar affection toward fascism. In recognition of this kind of alliance, as well as of the power in the hands of experts in the system envisaged by Ferri, it has been argued that the tenets of the Positive School carry political implications and inevitably drive toward centralized state power. See Caldwell, *Criminology*, note 14, pp. 433–36.

18. See Stephen Schafer, *Restitution to Victims of Crime* (London: Stevens and Sons, 1960) and *Correctional Research*, Bulletin No. 16, Nov. 1966, United Prison Association of Massachusetts, Boston.

19. Edward Shils, "The Calling of Sociology," in *Theories of Society*, Vol. II, ed. Talcott Parsons, et al. (New York: Free Press, 1961), p. 1447.

ENRICO FERRI: PIONEER IN CRIMINOLOGY (1856–1929)

THORSTEN SELLIN

W HEN Enrico Ferri died on April 12, 1929, one of the most colorful influential figures in the history of criminology disappeared. Born at San Benedetto Po in the province of Mantua on February 25, 1856, his active life spanned more than half a century, beginning with the publication of his dissertation in 1878 and ending with the fifth edition of his *Criminal Sociology*, which was being printed when he died. During the intervening five decades he became the acknowledged leader of the so-called positive school of criminal science, a highly successful trial lawyer, and perhaps Italy's greatest contemporary forensic orator; in addition, he was at various times throughout his life a member

Professor Sellin is emeritus professor of sociology, University of Pennsylvania; editor of the Annals of the American Academy of Political and Social Science (since 1929); and past president of the International Society of Criminology (1957-1966).

of Parliament, editor of the Socialist newspaper *Avanti*, indefatigable public lecturer, university professor, author of highly esteemed scholarly works, founder of a great legal journal, and a tireless polemicist in defense of his ideas. His was a rich and varied life, to which no brief article can do justice.

In *Principles of Criminal Law*,[1] a work which contained the systematic presentation of the legal principles of the positive school, Ferri listed what he himself regarded as his most important contributions. They were the demonstration that the concept of freedom of will has no place in criminal law and that social defense is the purpose of criminal justice; the three factors in crime causation; the classification of criminals in five classes; penal substitutes as a means of indirect social defense; motivation, rather than the objective nature of the crime, as the basis for sanctions; the demand that farm colonies be substituted for cellular isolation of prisoners by day; the indeterminate sentence instead of the dosage by fixed terms of institutionalization; the demand that hospitals for the criminal insane be established; the abolition of the jury; stress on the use of indemnification as a sanction in public law; and the principle that the crime must be studied in the offender.

Other observers have been inclined to add to this list his invention of the term "born criminal," the introduction of the concept of legal rather than moral responsibility, his pioneer work in establishing criminal sociology, and his propaganda for the scientific training of judges and correctional personnel.

One manner (usually chosen for a brief biography) of dealing with the work of Enrico Ferri is to pass quickly over his personal life and indicate systematically the nature of his scientific and philosophical contributions in their final form. But anyone who has immersed himself in the writings of and about Ferri would agree that Ferri the man is as fascinating as Ferri the scholar. Therefore, in this article I shall attempt both to tell the story of his life and to show the gradual development of

1. *Principii di diritto criminale* (Torino: UTET, 1928).

his thinking on criminological and criminal law problems, especially during his youth and early manhood.

* * *

Ferri was the son of a poor shopkeeper.[2] His early education was somewhat perturbed—private tutoring for two years, then two years at a school in Mantua, where he "learned nothing," failure in an examination when he tried to jump a school year, transfer to another school where he was almost expelled for truancy (he had become a bicycle enthusiast), removal from school by his father, who threatened to put him to manual labor, repentance after a week and return to the *ginnasio*, where shortly he took a successful final examination qualifying him to enter the *Liceo Virgilio* in Mantua.

At the Liceo, he made a beginning at finding himself. Not yet sixteen, he fell under the influence of a great teacher, Roberto Ardigò, who had just published a book, *Psychology as a Positive Science*, and had left his clerical robe to devote himself to independent philosophical study. The adolescent Ferri found in Ardigò's lectures a brain food "which decided my scientific orientation for the rest of my life."[3] Among other subjects, he made a fine record in mathematics and showed an interest in Latin; he simply ignored the requirement in Greek and was forced to "cheat" in his final examination for the diploma.[4]

Ferri now enrolled at the University of Bologna, where he was to spend three years. The first two of them were evidently

2. Biographical details have been garnered from the book by Ferri's disciple and co-worker Bruno Franchi, *Enrico Ferri, il noto, il mal noto, e l'ignorato* (Torino: Bocca, 1908), and from autobiographical notes frequently found scattered in Ferri's writings.

3. Ferri often acknowledged Ardigò's influence, especially in a brief article, "Ricordi liceali," which he contributed to a volume in honor of his teacher in 1898 and reprinted in his *Studi sulla criminalità ed altri saggi* (Torino: Bocca, 1901), pp. 474-77. See also his commemorative article "Roberto Ardigò," published after Ardigò's suicide in 1920 in *La Scuola Positiva*, Vol. 11, ser. 3, 1920, 289-94.

4. His stratagem apparently evoked no moral indignation, for in later life Ferri told the story publicly. In his defense speech in a forgery case

much devoted to extracurricular student activities. He attended the lectures in legal medicine and in criminal law, the latter given by Pietro Ellero, a prominent representative of the so-called "classical school." The third year he settled down to serious study. It was then he conceived a thesis in which he tried to demonstrate that the concept of free will, implicit in the current criminal law, was a fiction, and that the pretended moral responsibility of a criminal based on that fiction should give way to the concept of social or legal responsibility. Almost every person, he declared, regardless of his nature, was "socially accountable" for his actions by the fact that he was a member of society—not because he was capable of willing the illegal act. The thesis was brilliantly defended in 1877 and won him a scholarship.

He had struck his first blow at the theories of the classical school and proceeded promptly to spend the next academic year at the University of Pisa, where the acknowledged master and leader of the traditional philosophy of criminal law, Francesco Carrara, held the chair in that subject. Ferri attended lectures, argued with everybody about his ideas (he was nicknamed "free will Ferri"), and practiced his own system of elocution in preparation for a teaching career. Later he referred to these exercises in the following words: "At Pisa I did not as yet think of the bar, being all immersed in the thought of gaining a university chair in spite of my scientific heterodoxy. But in the interest of this future chair I felt a need to engage in pulmonary gymnastics, make speaking easy, and acquire the habit of order and clarity of exposition. I forced myself daily—at spots removed from the traffic on the beaches, along the Arno outside

---

in 1923, while discussing signatures, he mentioned how he invented his own characteristic one. "During the examination for the liceal diploma, I made a show of writing the paper in Greek, which I did not know and which was written by my very dear fellow-student Achille Loria. To distract the professor's attention, I began writing my name in various ways and finally in the manner I have since repeated for fifty years." See his *Difese penali* (3d ed., 3 vols.; Milano: UTET, 1925), Vol. II, 686. Ferri had reciprocated by writing Loria's examination in mathematics.

the city—to talk aloud for an hour at a stretch, improvising on some topic which I picked at random from a number of cards that I had prepared and put into my pocket before leaving home."[5]

Part of the year was spent in revising his dissertation and preparing it for the printer. Before the end of the term, Carrara, who must have regarded his twenty-year-old opponent with a mixture of amusement and irritation, and who once exclaimed that "instead of learning from us Ferri has come to teach us," permitted him to deliver a lecture on criminal attempts from the point of view of the "newer ideas." It was to be the first of many, for three years before his death, he estimated that he had by then delivered some 2,300 university lectures and over 600 public lectures of a scientific nature (on some 40 topics), not counting addresses in court and thousands of political speeches.[6]

When he published his dissertation in the summer of 1878,[7] he sent a copy to Lombroso, who had just brought out the second edition of his *Criminal Man*. Years later, Ferri reported that Lombroso "responded in an encouraging and congratulatory manner, but . . . gave our mutual friend Filippo Turati . . . the following appraisal of my book, in which I explicitly affirmed my intention to apply the positive method to the science of criminal law: 'Ferri isn't positivist enough!' I remember that at that time, burdened as I was by a remnant of scholastic and metaphysical concepts (because of which, as Garofalo said, and as I have since declared and demonstrated in successive publications, my theory of imputability was little in harmony with the preceding negation of free will and with the beginning renovation of the criminal law) Lombroso's opinion seemed to me inexact and exaggerated. And I wrote to Turati: 'What,! Does

5. *Difese penali*, Vol. II, 5.
6. Cited by Teresa Labriola in an article, "Enrico Ferri," in *Scritti in onore di Enrico Ferri per il cinquantesimo anno di suo insegnamento universitario* (Torino: UTET, 1929), p. 265.
7. *La negazione del libero arbitrio e la teorica dell'imputabilità.*

Lombroso suggest that I, a lawyer, should go and measure the heads of criminals in order to be positivist enough?!' "[8]

Within a few years, Ferri would answer that question of his in the affirmative, but at the moment he was getting ready to leave for France, having won a travelling fellowship by his dissertation. He was to spend a year in Paris. He had set for himself the task of making a study of the trends and characteristics of criminality in France during half a century, using the data of the judicial criminal statistics which had been appearing since 1826, and which had been little exploited by scholars since the early days of Quetelet and Guerry.

The collection of the data for his project absorbed a great deal of his time, but he also studied German at Melzi's institute (he never really learned English), attended the lectures of Laboulaye, political theorist, and Quatrefages, physical anthropologist, and wrote a lengthy review of Lombroso's book. In November, 1878, he sent the review to the *Rivista Europea* which published it.[9]

He commended Lombroso for having "gone in search of the characteristics that should reveal to us . . . the habitual, incorrigible criminal, who is such . . . because of the inexorable tyranny of his own organic constitution, inherited from his ancestors; a criminal who persists in evil . . . and who is not reformable by the old spiritualistic systems, according to which man commits a crime or is good, reforms or relapses solely by the fiat of his own will and not due to the necessary effect of the conditions in which he is placed by a given environment." He was especially pleased to see so many case histories in the book, for they provided "a vivid scientific material for any one who wants to search for general juridical principles, not in abstractions of metaphysical character but in the study of those

8. Enrico Ferri, "Polemica in difesa della scuola criminale positiva" (1886). Reprinted in *Studi sulla criminalità ed altri saggi*, pp. 234–329. On page 245 appears an extract from a symposium with the same title, of which he, Lombroso, Garofalo, and Fioretti were co-authors.

9. "Studi Critici su *L'Uomo delinquente* del Prof. C. Lombroso." Reprinted in *Studi sulla criminalità ed altri saggi*, pp. 1–12.

living beings who, while absent from all ancient and modern treatises of criminal law encounter us at every step in the courts of assizes and the lower courts. He [Lombroso] thus offers us a first ray of light to dispel the most serious contradictions at least, which in practice always arise between the conclusions of psychiatry and the so-called eternal verities of an aprioristic criminal science."

As for the statement by Lombroso that crime is a natural necessity—a statement which had caused his critics to point out that one could hardly punish a person unless one assumed his moral responsibility—Ferri simply replied that Lombroso had been grossly misunderstood. Crime is not a social need but is inevitable in society. But equally inevitable is the law, because society believes that punishments are necessary and inevitable for its protection. Since society has the right to defend itself against aggressors, it has the right to punish. That is all there is to justice. Justice is the will of the majority, which considers a given provision necessary. "When an institution is desired by the majority of the citizens as being necessary for the public welfare, it is—and only because of this—just." Ferri was to be quite consistent in holding this view. Toward the end of his life it helped him to come to terms with fascism and even to accept, within certain limits, the death penalty to which he had been a lifelong opponent.

If Ferri had not been a complete positivist when he left Italy, his stay in France completed his education. He later looked upon his study of the French criminal statistics and his attendance at the lectures of Quatrefages as a "healthful naturalistic bath from which I issued a true and convinced positivist." It is not that he accepted the positivistic philosophy in toto, but that he would from then on repeatedly declare that the "experimental," i.e., inductive method of investigation, the method of Galileo and Bacon, was the only one that would yield knowledge that would permit a nation to deal intelligently with the problem of crime.

It is not surprising that Ferri went to the University of Turin the following year: Lombroso was professor of legal medicine there. Some time before he left Paris in the spring of 1879, Ferri had asked the Council of Higher Education in Rome for a license as titular docent in criminal law and had also applied to the University of Turin for a docentship in criminal procedure with the right to hold examinations. To qualify for this latter position he lectured on the jury system before the examining committee. He remained a consistent opponent to jury trials for ordinary crimes, for in a scientifically oriented court procedure, judges trained in the social and psychological sciences would be better able to dispose of offenders properly. The lecture, which won him the docentship, grew into a celebrated monograph published late in 1880.

In the Council at Rome, Ferri's application faced tough opposition. One very influential Council member, averse to his views, nearly defeated his application, but finally he received his license and promptly afterward gave his introductory lecture at the University on "Penal Substitutes."[10] By this term he meant all the social measures, including non-criminal legislation, which a nation might take in order to prevent crime and thereby reduce the need for criminal sanctions. It was in this lecture that he stated what he called his law of criminal saturation, according to which the level of a country's criminality is determined by factors in the social environment and changes when they change.

Ferri completed his analysis of the French data and prepared a manuscript for publication while he was in Turin.[11] He had begun that research because he recognized that Lombroso's studies, which had been largely limited to habitual and insane prisoners, dealt with only a narrow aspect of the problem of criminality. "Crime," Ferri said, "like every other human action, is the effect of multiple causes, which, although always interlaced in an indissoluble net, can nevertheless be separated for

10. "Dei sostitutivi penali," *Archivio di psichiatria*, Vol. 1, 1880.
11. "Studi sulla criminalità in Francia del 1826 al 1878, secondo i dati contenuti nei *Comptes généraux de l'administration de la Justice criminelle*," *Annali di statistica*, Vol. 21, ser. 2, 1881. Reprinted in *Studi sulla criminalità ed altri saggi*, pp. 17–59. Citations are to the reprint.

research purposes. The factors of crime are anthropological or individual, physical or telluric, and social. Anthropological factors are: the offender's age, sex, civil status, occupation, residence, social class, degree of training and education, organic and mental constitution. Physical factors are: race, climate, fertility and distribution of soil, the daily cycle, the seasons, the meteorological factors, the annual temperature. Social factors are: increase or decrease of population, migration, public opinion, customs and religion, the nature of the family; political, financial and commercial life; agricultural and industrial production and distribution; public administration of safety, education and welfare; penal and civil legislation, in general."[12]

He chose the social factors for investigation for two good reasons: the scope of the investigation of the "phenomenon of crime" needed to be widened, and these factors had a more direct relationship with sociology and legislative practice. Even when the legislator in this area of "social pathology" had some understanding of the importance of anthropological and physical factors there was little he could do to modify them; social factors could be influenced because they were more tractable. His findings convinced him of the wisdom of his judgment, for he arrived at the conclusion that criminality had shown an enormous increase (i.e., total criminality, divided into offenses against persons, property and public order) in France, and at the conviction that since both physical and anthropological factors undergo relatively minor changes in time, changes in the social environment must have been responsible for the increase.[13]

This first empirical study by Ferri, begun in a positivistic spirit and pursued with great skill, was very well received. He was soon after (1882) appointed by the Minister of Justice,

12. *Ibid.*, p. 18.
13. Two decades later, Ferri added a footnote to the reprinted study, in which he congratulated himself on having stressed the importance of social factors as early as in 1880. This, he said, proved that Italian and French critics, who claimed that the positive school dealt only with anthropological factors, were wrong. It also served "to explain the logical evolution of my thinking, which has gradually, but on the basis of scientific research in the

Zanardelli, a member of the Commission on Judicial and Notarial Statistics and remained in this position for a dozen years.

Ferri had gone to Turin because of his belief that "in order to formulate principles concerning crimes, penalties, and criminals, it is first necessary to study . . . criminals and prisons," since facts should precede theories. "I therefore went for a year to Turin to study with Lombroso and, as his student, visited prisons, mental hospitals, and laboratories."[14] It was the year in which Lombroso started to edit his periodical, the *Archivio di psichiatria*. Ferri contributed to its first volume not only his lecture on penal substitutes but also a paper on the relationship of criminal anthropology and criminal law,[15] which contained what he always regarded as one of his basic ideas, a scientific classification of criminals which would serve as the basis for a rational system of sanctions. In presenting this classification, consisting of five classes, he coined the term "born criminal" to designate the atavistic type which Lombroso believed he had identified. The classification included "(1) the born or instinctive criminal, who carries from birth, through unfortunate heredity from his progenitors (criminals, alcoholics, syphilitics, subnormals, insane, neuropathics, etc.) a reduced resistance to criminal stimuli and also an evident and precocious propensity to crime; (2) the insane criminal, affected by a clinically identified mental disease or by a neuropsychopathic condition which groups him with the mentally diseased; (3) the passional criminal, who, in two varieties, the criminal through passion (a prolonged and chronic mental state) or through emotion (explosive and unexpected mental state), represents a type at the opposite pole from the criminal due to congenital tendencies and, besides having good personal antecedents, has a normal moral character, even though he is nervously very excitable; (4) the occasional crim-

---

field of both general and of criminal sociology, arrived at the ultimate consequences of socialistic doctrines." *Ibid.*, p. 19.

14. "Polemica in difesa della scuola criminale positiva," *loc. cit.*

15. "Dei limiti fra diritto penale ed antropologia criminale," *Archivio di psichiatria*, Vol. 1, 1880–81, 444 ff.

inal who constitutes the majority of lawbreakers and is the product of family and social milieu more than of abnormal personal physico–mental conditions, and therefore has psychological traits less deviating from those of the social class to which he belongs; (5) the habitual criminal, or rather, the criminal by acquired habit, who is mostly a product of the social environment in which, due to abandonment by his family, lack of education, poverty, bad companions in urban centers, already in his childhood begins as an occasional offender; add to this his moral deformation, caused or not hindered by contemporary prison systems where he enters into contacts with other and worse criminals in the prisons, as well as the difficulties of social readaption once he has served his term, and he will acquire the habit of criminality and, besides constant recidivism, may actually come to make crime a trade."[16]

Ferri did not believe that every criminal always fitted completely into his classification. Classes do not exist in nature, he said, but they are a necessary instrument by which the human mind can better understand the multiform reality of things. In daily life, criminals would often not appear so well defined as the classification suggested. Rather, a judge would find that the defendant would present mixed characteristics. This realization was to cause Ferri, in a near future, to study the murderer with greater care in order to acquire knowledge about aggressive dangerous criminals that would aid judges in identifying them as such.

The classification remained unchanged in Ferri's mind for most of his life. In fact, his addition of a sixth class in the fifth edition of his *Sociologia Criminale* (1929–30) appears to have been a kind of afterthought which, although clear, was so poorly integrated that he forgot or had no time to revise other sections of his book that still mentioned only five classes. Even his co-worker, Arturo Santoro, who had seen his book through press,

16. As elaborated in his *L'Omicida nella psicologia e nella psicopatologia criminale* (2d ed.), and in *L'Omicidio–Suicidio; responsabilità giuridica* (5th ed.; Torino: UTET, 1925), pp. 54–55.

later mentions only the five classes in his biography of Ferri. Yet, in the work just mentioned, Ferri said: "To these five categories of voluntary criminals it is necessary to add a class, which is becoming more and more numerous in our mechanical age and in the vertiginous speed of modern life, namely the involuntary criminals. . . . They are pseudo-criminals who cause damage and peril by their lack of foresight, imprudence, negligence or disobedience of regulations rather than through malice, and they represent various degrees of dangerousness." Some of them have a weak sense of moral sensitivity, some of them lack technical knowledge, some are inattentive, and others are exhausted.[17]

Between Ferri and Lombroso (twenty years his senior) there began a deep and lasting friendship marked by mutual respect and profit to both, for while Ferri owed much of his system of ideas to the stimulation of Lombroso, he also became the catalyst who synthesized the latter's concepts with those of the sociologist and had no little influence on Lombroso's thinking.

Ferri stayed but a year in Turin. Pietro Ellero had been appointed a justice of the Supreme Court and before he left his chair at Bologna he expressed the desire that Ferri be appointed as his successor. Ferri thus returned to his alma mater as professor of criminal law three years after receiving his degree. In December 1880, before he was twenty-five years old, he held his introductory lecture on the subject of "the new horizons in criminal law and procedure." One present described it as one of those events "that are epoch-making in university annals." The young professor "spoke impassionately for two hours, with growing enthusiasm, irresistibly. Borne upon impetuous waves of eloquence were the daring, magnificent, and original ideas dressed in a limpid, imaginative, exact, and always challenging prose."[18] It was this lecture which grew into his best known work, *Criminal Sociology*.[19]

17. *Sociologia criminale* (5th ed.), Vol. II, 295-96.
18. Quoted in Franchi, *Enrico Ferri*, p. 94.
19. The first and second editions of 1881 and 1884 carried the title *I nuovi orrizonti del diritto e della procedura penale*. The third edition, with

Ferri was a born and imaginative teacher. He began at Bologna a plan which he continued to follow later in teaching criminal law—he took his students on a tour of penal institutions and mental hospitals, true to his belief that the future system of criminal justice must be administered by people who have a knowledge of the criminal.

In the fall of 1881 he began a study of 699 prisoners in the prisons of Castelfranco Emilia and Pesaro, 301 insane in the mental hospital of Bologna, and 711 soldiers in the military barracks of Bologna, the soldiers being a control group so selected that they would belong to the same sections of Italy from which the experimental groups came. The research was

---

the title of *Sociologia criminale,* was issued in 1892. (Ferri had defined the term "criminal sociology" in an article published in 1882.) In the preface Ferri observed that the new title was more in harmony with the content of the book and he characterized the opus as "a work of propaganda and an elementary guide for anyone who intends to dedicate himself to the scientific study of offenders and of the means of prevention and social defense against them. Hence the almost superabundant citations and the voluminous bibliography." The fourth edition came in 1900; in it he claimed that he had examined all the literature of the previous decade to complete his documentation. The fifth and final edition was published in two volumes, the first in 1929 and the second in 1930, posthumously. Arturo Santoro, who had been assisting Ferri, and who had been asked to complete the footnotes, wrote the preface and saw the work through to publication. It seems clear that in the nearly three decades between the last two editions, Ferri had found less and less time to keep up with the literature, except that of his own country. Of the approximately 4,700 footnote references in the fifth edition fewer than 1,100 date from this century and 75 percent of these are to Italian sources, compared with 48 percent of the references to works published before 1900. Ferri used to say during his later years that he found nothing written of such importance that it had caused him to change his views.

Translations of this or that edition were published in different countries. A partial translation into English of the third edition appeared in a "Criminology Series," edited by a British clergyman, W. Douglas Morrison (*Criminal Sociology,* London and New York: Appleton, 1896) who, according to Ferri, omitted the entire first section of the work because it was too heterodox. The American Institute of Criminal Law and Criminology sponsored a translation of the fourth edition (*Criminal Sociology,* Boston: Little, Brown, 1917).

based on individual case studies. He assembled as much information about each individual as possible from the institution's records, observed each prisoner discretely in his cell or in the prison yard, interviewed him and examined him for about half an hour, on the average, one part of the examination being somatic, the other psychological. Out of this research, which occupied him intensively for three years, grew his monograph on homicide–suicide and his work on homicide, both of them important.[20]

He finally also "measured the heads of criminals!" A few years later, in 1886, he was to write: "Having digested and assimilated some kilograms of criminal statistics and added some anthropological researches, I believed that I had gained an adequate enough concept of reality to be able to undertake the construction of a truly positive legal system. That is what I am now doing with the monograph on homicide, studied both naturalistically and juridically, at which I have been working for three years (because positivistic studies are slower and more difficult than the construction of fantastic syllogisms) and which will be, I hope, an eloquent response, for my part, to the minute criticisms now being directed at us even though the scientific edifice of the new school is unfinished (we have worked at it only seven years). . . . Then I also understood clearly what Lombroso meant by his opinion of my first book and therefore I now understand the psychological state of mind and the intellectual phase in which our critics find themselves, for at that time, I too did not have that scientific

20. Already cited. The monograph on homicide–suicide appeared first serially in 1883–84 in the *Archivio di psichiatria e scienze penali* and in book form in 1884, 1892, and 1925. The monograph on homicide was not published until 1895; the second edition of 1925 omitted all the anthropological and statistical data, which occupied 216 pages in the first edition, together with several hundred pages of graphic material. The second edition was entirely devoted to the psychology and psychopathology of the homicide and was frankly addressed to judges, prosecutors, and defense attorneys. For a comment on the first edition, see H. Zimmern, "Enrico Ferri on Homicide," *Popular Science Monthly*, Vol. 49, Sept.–Oct. 1896, 678–84, 828–37.

attitude, which can only be acquired by the methodical examination of facts."[21]

He had already left Bologna, before the works just mentioned were seen in print. In 1882, he accepted a chair at the University of Siena, where he remained for four years. This was a fruitful period of teaching and study. Papers on "the right to punish as a social function" (in which his concept of legal responsibility took final form), "the positive school of criminal law," "collective property and the class struggle," and "socialism and criminality" were written. The book on homicide-suicide was published, as well as a second edition of his *New Horizons*. The International Prison Congress, in 1885, and the simultaneous first Congress of Criminal Anthropology gave him an opportunity to present his views on prison reform in an address on the cellular (i.e., Pennsylvanian) system and the labor of prisoners, in which he condemned the cellular system as the greatest mistake of the century.

But, he was soon to leave, for a long time, the calm atmosphere of the university. In the province of Mantua a large group of peasants were being prosecuted for incitement to civil war, the case having grown out of certain troubles between them and their landlords. Ferri was engaged as one of their defense attorneys. His brilliant socio-economic address to the court secured their acquittal.[22] Two months later, in May 1886, Mantua elected him a deputy to the national Parliament, where he was to sit, through eleven re-elections, until 1924, representing various boroughs of the country.

The election was a personal victory, because Ferri carried no party label. His studies had brought him close to socialism, but the brand of naive utopian socialism current in Italy did not appeal to his rational mind. He had at various times pointed out to those who claimed a socialist society would eliminate crime that crime is an inevitable phenomenon and

21. "Polemica in difesa della scuola criminale positiva," *loc. cit.*
22. "I contadini Mantovani al processo di Venezia imputati di 'eccitamento alla guerra civile,' " *Difese penali*, Vol. I, 85–156.

that every society, whatever its nature, had its own forms of criminality. Where in a feudal society crimes against the person dominated, in a capitalistic society, crimes of theft and fraud prevailed; in a socialist society, new forms would arise. His Mantuan defense speech revealed how far he had progressed toward a consistent Marxism. At least, it revealed it to Ferri himself who, after re-reading it in 1925, said that doing so made him realize "that already then, in 1886, I was a Marxist without knowing it. The speech is, in fact, completely oriented toward historical materialism (which I have called economic determinism) by means of which it can be demonstrated that historical individual and social facts are the direct or indirect product of the underlying and determining economic conditions of the individual and the collectivity."[23]

Now the Ferris moved to Rome. (In 1884 he had married a Florentine woman, Camilla Guarnieri, a marriage which proved most successful from all points of view and was to give him two sons and a daughter.) In Parliament Ferri attached himself to the radical liberals. He had given up his chair at Siena but continued to teach in Rome as a "libero docente." He also wrote about the positive school and its mission, began to increase his fame as a trial lawyer, and started to organize labor cooperatives among the poverty-stricken agricultural workers of Mantua. In 1890, he was—miracle of miracles—called to succeed Francesco Carrara at the University of Pisa, but he was to hold the chair only three years, because Marxian doctrines were becoming known in Italy and he was led, partly by his philosophy of economic determinism and partly by his loyalty to his constituents who were being drawn into the newly organized (1892) Italian Socialist Labor Party, to join the Party in 1893. This act led to the loss of his professorship.

The family now moved to San Dominico, near Fiesole, where he was to live for several years. Life was becoming more and more hectic. Ferri soon discovered the weakness of

23. *Ibid.,* p. 8.

the Party in Parliament and threw himself into the task of educating the masses. Franchi claims that during twenty years Ferri spent 200 out of 365 nights in a pullman sleeper. He became the people's orator, par excellence, lecturing on some 40 topics of scientific, historical, economic, and sociological character. There was no village in Italy where he had not been at least once; the urbanites heard him more often. In 1896 when the National Socialist Congress decided to start a party newspaper, it was Ferri who went out on a three weeks' lecture tour to collect the necessary 10,000 lire. Later, during a brief period, he edited *Avanti*.

In Parliament he achieved nationwide attention on more than one occasion, but especially when he led a filibuster against the government in 1899 and particularly when he campaigned for an investigation of graft in the Navy Department. That experience (1903–1906) involved him in lawsuits. He was even sentenced to eleven months in prison in a criminal libel suit brought by the Minister of the Navy, but Parliament finally set up an investigating commission, which discovered that the charges made by Ferri were true. He was openly praised in Parliament, the sentence against him was dropped, and he was called, in 1906,[24] to succeed Impallomeni as professor of criminal law at the University of Rome. He had been a candidate for this chair and for professorships at other universities several times during the previous decade, but had always been bypassed because of his political views and the government's preference for more traditional ideas on criminal law, although he had, as already mentioned, been lecturing as a "libero docente." He had also given lecture courses at the University of Brussels every other year from 1895 to 1903, and at the School of Advanced Social Studies in Paris in 1889 and 1901, not to mention a lecture tour at Dutch and Flemish universities.

24. It was during this period that portraits of Ferri appeared in American magazines. See *Munsey's*, Vol. 26, Mar. 1902, 829; *World To-day*, Vol. 9, Aug. 1905, 876; *Outlook*, Vol. 85, May 23, 1907, 692.

His campaign for the reform of the criminal law had suffered nothing in the meanwhile. In 1892, Ferri had founded a legal journal, *La Scuola Positiva*. This gave the positivists an organ of their own, in which they could propagate their ideas. The journal became a worthy opponent to Luigi Lucchini's *Rivista Penale*, chief organ of the classicists, and complemented Lombroso's *Archivio*. He remained editor, or chief of the editorial board, until his death, though he had many collaborators and associates.

In 1908, Ferri went to South America on a lecture tour, giving 80 lectures in 110 days. The tour was evidently handled by some impressario and the topics were chosen to appeal to a lay public. His success was phenomenal. Two years later he returned there at the invitation of universities, and lectured to professional audiences. He died before he could realize his ambition to lecture in the United States.[25]

His views also became well known abroad due to his participation in nearly all international congresses of criminal anthropology and in many similar congresses of the International Criminalistic Society (now the International Association of Criminal Law); of the International Prison Congresses he attended one in Rome in 1865, and one in London in 1925.

The positive school placed great emphasis on trained judges and the professionalization of all who dealt with crime or criminals. In 1912 Ferri founded, in Rome, a School for Ap-

---

25. In addition to his *Criminal Sociology*, translated into English in 1896 and 1917, a few books and articles by Ferri appeared in the United States. The books were *Socialism and Modern Science: Darwin, Spencer, Marx* (New York: International Library, 1900), and *The Positive School of Criminology* (Chicago: Charles H. Kerr, 1906). An article, "The Delinquent in Art and Literature" appeared in the *Atlantic*, Vol. 60, Aug. 1897, 233-40, and the following appeared in the *Journal of Criminal Law and Criminology*: "Present Movement in Criminal Anthropology" (Part 2 of a symposium on Charles Goring's *The English Convict*), Vol. 5, July 1914, 224-27; "Nomination of a Commission for the Positivist Reform of the Italian Criminal Code," Vol. 11, May 1920, 67-76; "Reform of Penal Law in Italy," Vol. 12, Aug. 1921, 178-98; "A Character Study and Life History of Violet Gibson, who attempted the life of Benito Mussolini, on the 7th of April, 1926," Vol. 19, Aug. 1928, 11-19.

plied Criminal Law and Procedure (*Scuola di applicazione giuridico-criminale*) which drew many students, even from abroad.

Finally, at the end of the First World War, it seemed that the time of harvest had arrived for the positivists. In 1919, the Minister of Justice, Ludovico Mortara, one of Ferri's schoolmates in the Liceo at Mantua, invited him to take the presidency of a commission that would prepare a project of a criminal code to replace the one of 1889. The Commission was to have a membership drawn from all the various "schools" of thinking on such matters, but in the end, as a result of resignations, it came to represent mostly a positivistic orientation. The resulting project was presented in 1921 and is the greatest achievement of the positivists, even though it contained some compromises. It was translated into several languages, including English, and was widely distributed.[26] John H. Wigmore, to cite but one example, wrote Ferri on April 17, 1921: "I am happy to have received the Italian project. It is a masterpiece, even judging from a cursory examination. What a marvelous reward for your patient, brilliant apostolate, which has permitted you to translate your ideas into a code! I hope that the Parliament will approve this project."

This hope was not fulfilled. Postwar Italy became more and more unsettled. The Fascist revolution succeeded because the government was unable to cope with the country's economic and social problems. Ferri had left the Socialist Party before the war and in 1924 he was to close his parliamentary career by refusing re-election. His attempts to save his Project failed; the need for a new code was to be filled by one drafted by the new government. Ferri was made a member of the commission which, in 1927, presented a project which was adopted in 1930. In the fifth edition of his *Criminal Sociology*, in connection with a discussion on the need for social reforms

26. "Relazione sul Progetto preliminare di Codice Penale Italiano" (Libro I), *La Scuola Positiva*, N.S. 1, 1921, 1–130. The project itself follows on pages 131–156.

that would eliminate poverty and other social evils, he wrote
in a footnote: "While in the 4th edition (1900) I alluded
hopefully to socialist trends—to which I have given my fervid
enthusiasm, especially by the propaganda I have carried on
for the moral and social education of the Italian masses—now
in the 5th edition (1929) I have to note with regard to
Italy that since the influence of the Socialist Party disappeared
after the war, because it neither knew how to make a revolution nor wanted to assume the responsibility of power, the
task of the social prevention of criminality was assumed and
has begun to be realized by the Fascist government, which
both in the Rocco Project of a Penal Code and in many
special statutes has accepted and is putting into effect some
of the principles and the most characteristic practical proposals
of the positive school."[27] In theory, he objected to many
concepts in the Rocco project, which carried the stamp of
the middle-of-the-road school of thinking of the neoclassicists,
but as a practical man he viewed it as a step in the right
direction and as a partial victory for his idea. As for Fascism,
he saw something of value in it, so far as criminal justice
was concerned, because it represented to him a systematic
reaffirmation of the authority of the State against the excesses
of individualism, which he had always criticized.

His last years were devoted chiefly to the work which was
to contain the entire legal formulation of positivistic thought
in the field of criminal law. He had for nearly fifty years
taught this subject and out of this teaching grew his *Principles
of Criminal Law*, which he sent to the printer the summer
before he died. He was also working on the final revision of
his *Criminal Sociology* and had just completed it at his death.
A month before that event he had been nominated senator,
but his confirmation never took place.

An activity as varied and rich as Ferri's could be exercised

27. *Sociologia Criminale*, Vol. I, 11-12. See also his "Fascismo e Scuola
Positiva nella difesa sociale contro la criminalità," *La Scuola Positiva*, N.S.
6, 1926, 241-74.

only by a man whose life was well organized. He reserved his mornings from seven to half past twelve for his authorship —the preparation of books, articles, briefs, etc. In the afternoon he read professional literature, made notes for future use, and took care of his correspondence. He never worked after eight in the evening and went to bed after his evening meal. He was abstemious, never smoked, believed in physical exercise and manual labor, which he took some opportunity to engage in during his vacations. In the summer he usually took his family to different parts of Italy so that his children would become acquainted with them. During these periods he rested from all work as much as possible. In August and September he travelled to international congresses. He did not go to the theater or concerts; they interfered with his sleep.

As he became more and more famous as a lawyer, he learned more and more about the practice of advocacy. The lengthy prefaces to the editions of his *Difese penali,* a veritable case book for the aspiring trial lawyer, are a manual on the art of the advocate, telling him not only how to prepare and develop an oration but advising him on the personal hygiene of the orator.

* * *

Ferri's system of ideas has been at least partially evoked in the preceding pages. A remarkable fact is that his basic philosophy of criminal justice and most of his fundamental concepts had been formulated and stated in various publications by the time he was 26 years old. Looking backward, he was able to say, in the preface to his collected essays in 1901, that he was fortunate in that his "early theoretical and practical conclusions were firm, for while their integration has inevitably evolved and been completed and corrected in some details, they have remained basically unchanged."

Ferri was essentially a legal reformer. His solid contributions to the study of the etiology of criminal conduct were incidental means for achieving a greater understanding of the course which the reformation of criminal justice should take.

33

A broad vein of practicality ran through all his work; a desire to achieve a demonstrably effective criminal justice, which would afford maximum protection or defense of society against the criminal.

The "positive school," of which Ferri was the chief architect, stood in clear opposition to traditional, "classical" criminal jurisprudence. Historically, the principal reason for the rise of a positivistic view of criminal justice was the necessity to put a stop to the exaggerated individualism in favor of the criminal in order to obtain a greater respect for the rights of honest people who constitute the great majority.[28] Practically, "the positive school consists of the following: study first the natural origin of crime and then its social and legal consequences in order to provide, by social and legal means, the various remedies which will have the greatest effect on the various causes that produce it. This is our assumption, this the innovation we have made, not so much in our particular conclusions as in our research method."[29] Ferri repeatedly contrasted this mode of thinking with that of the "classical school." In 1886 he said, in a polemic against the critics of that persuasion who were attacking the new movement, "Very well, what can we positivists do against such critics? Frankly speaking, nothing. We speak two different languages. For us, the experimental [inductive] method is the key to all knowledge; to them everything derives from logical deductions and traditional opinion. For them, facts should give place to syllogisms; for us the fact governs and no reasoning can occur without starting with facts; for them science needs only paper, pen, and ink and the rest comes from a brain stuffed with more or less abundant reading of books made with the same ingredients. For us science requires spending a long time in examining facts one by one, evaluating them, reducing them to a common denominator, extracting the central idea from

28. Preface to the Spanish edition of the *New Horizons*. Reprinted in *Studi sulla criminalità ed altri saggi*, pp. 320–33, p. 324.
29. *Ibid.*, p. 323.

them. For them a syllogism or an anecdote suffices to demolish a myriad of facts gathered through years of observation and analysis; for us the reverse is true."[30]

The positive school cultivated a "science of criminality and of social defense against it." As Ferri conceived it, this discipline consisted of the scientific study of the crime (a) as an individual fact (somato-psychological condition of the offender) by anthropology, psychology, and criminal psychopathology; and (b) as a social fact (physical and social environmental conditions) by criminal statistics, monographic studies, and comparative ethnographic studies—for the purpose of systematizing social defense measures (a) of a preventive nature, either indirect or remote (through "penal substitutes") or direct or proximate (by the police); or (b) of a repressive nature through criminal law and procedure, techniques of prison treatment, and after-care. This science Ferri called criminal sociology. (His subordination of criminal law irritated his antagonists immensely; they preferred to look on the social and biological sciences as "auxiliary disciplines" of the criminal law.) Outside of criminal sociology lay certain other essential disciplines: criminal policy, i.e., the art of the legislator in adapting the defensive and repressive defense measures proposed by criminal sociology in a way to meet the exigencies of a given people; legislative technique, i.e., the actual drafting and adoption of legislation; penal jurisprudence, i.e., the art of judges and attorneys in using scientific ideas, such as bio-social data and juridical doctrines, in the interpretation of the criminal law and its application to the individual case.[31]

We have already noted that Ferri made original contributions both to the study of the crime as an "individual fact" by his researches on prisoners (which led to his works on homicide and suicide), and to the study of crime as a "social fact" by his studies of French criminal statistics in particular. His most important and lasting contribution was, however,

30. "Polemica in difesa della scuola criminale positiva," p. 244.
31. *Sociologia criminale* (5th ed.), Vol. II, 554-55.

his ideas concerning the reformation of the system of criminal justice, some of the most important of which will be mentioned here.

First, it would be necessary to abolish the concept of moral responsibility and replace it by one of legal or social responsibility. "The positive theory says: every man is always responsible to society for any crime he commits. Whether he is a juvenile, insane, drunk, or a sleep-walker, he should always be held responsible, i.e., subject to the consequences of his criminal act, when that act is contrary to public safety and forbidden by the criminal law. . . . There is no more or less of criminal responsibility; either one is responsible or not responsible (for legally justifiable reasons)."[32] Moral responsibility was to Ferri a metaphysical concept; it designated something which no one could measure adequately and led to the acquittal or the failure of prosecution of offenders who often were extremely dangerous to social safety. For him, social defense against the criminal required a system based on legal responsibility.

Moral responsibility having been eliminated, the consequences of crime for the convicted offender would no longer be retributive punishments (*pena-castigo*), but scientifically determined sanctions (*pena-difesa*) based on the degree of danger which the offender constituted for society and the degree to which his motives were blameworthy, rather than on the objective nature of his act. The function of the court would be to select the proper sanction for the convicted offender. To do so would require a great deal of understanding and knowledge on the part of the judges and prosecutors. In 1896 Ferri said, "The criminal justice of the future, administered by judges who have sufficient knowledge, not of Roman or civil law, but of psychology, anthropology, and psychiatry, will have for its sole task to determine if the defendant is the material author of the established crime; and instead of brilliant logomachies by the prosecution and the defense in an

32. "Il dolo criminoso," *Difese penali* (3d. ed.), Vol. III, 177.

effort to trick one another, there will be a scientific discussion on the personal and social condition of the offender in order to classify him in one or another anthropological class to which one or another form of indeterminate segregation will apply."[33]

Any attempt at real individualization of sentences by courts should be discouraged. He believed it utopian to think that any judge could make minute studies of every convicted offender. The judge should have enough scientific knowledge to permit him to place the offender in the proper class (i.e., in one of Ferri's five or six classes) and then assign the sanction proper to each class—the sanction might be a mere warning (judicial pardon), the payment of reparations (which Ferri believed to be adequate for a number of offenders), compulsory labor in freedom (the worker's wages being attached), or indeterminate commitment to a mental hospital for the criminal insane, a reformatory, an institution for alcoholics, an agricultural colony, etc. Individualization, beyond this point, should be left to those who execute sentences, but even then he was inclined to think that, considering the numbers involved, real individualization of treatment would remain an incompletely realizable hope. In the treatment of offenders after sentence the greatest effort should be made in the case of the occasional criminal; it was not really worth spending a great deal of effort on the mentally abnormal or the congenital offender.

As for those committed on indeterminate sentences to some form of institutionalization, a periodic revision of the sentence should occur. The criminal justice of the future would see the setting up of "permanent committees in which judges, prosecutors, defenders (who would also be public officials because it is absurd to consider the defense of a suspect as a private affair like the interpretation of a contract) and with

33. See "Il Congresso d'Antropologia Criminale a Ginevra," in *La Scuola Positiva*, Sept. 1896. Reprinted in *Studi sulla criminalità ed altri saggi*, pp. 216–33, p. 229.

them psychiatrists and anthropologists would examine periodically those committed, with the guarantee of publicity, to determine if the term should be prolonged or not."[34]

The state should also provide for after-care and supervision.

* * *

The influence of the positive school has been felt in Italy and throughout the world. The reforms made in the criminal law in all civilized nations in the last half century have resulted in the adoption of many of the proposals of the positivists. The entire European movement to provide so-called "security measures" parallel with or subsequent to "punishments" as means of dealing with habitual offenders, abnormal offenders, vagrants, etc., derives from the positivists, and the "social defense school" which has arisen in Europe since the last war owes its stimulus and many of its basic ideas to Ferri and his co-workers.[35]

Ferri remained until his death completely certain that regardless of what compromises might have to be made with more traditional views of criminal justice, his ideas would in the end be accepted as the most logical basis for social defense against crime. At the end of his preface to his treatise, *Principles of Criminal Law* (1928), he wrote: "Thus I close my scientific life, showing the juridical application of these doctrines, originally and obviously Italian, which in the last fifty years I have seen, after the early fearful anathemas, progressively adopted in all countries; this gives me a serene certainty that they will finally be completely realized."

A few months ago I drove along the Viale Ferri at Rocca di Papa, the picturesque hill town some twenty miles from Rome, where Ferri had a large villa from which he had a magnificent view to the west over the Roman campagna, Lake Albano, and Castelgandolfo. I first met him there in the fall of 1925 and still remember the courtesy and kindness he showed a young student. Some days later I heard him give the introductory

34. *Ibid.*
35. Marc Ancel, *La défense sociale nouvelle* (Paris: Editions Cujas, 1954).

lecture at the University of Rome—a report on the International Penal and Penitentiary Congress, which he had just attended in London. Slender of build, a head taller than most Italians, and with a shock of white curly hair and a white beard, he was an imposing figure and still possessed, at seventy, the clarity of exposition and the manner of the great orator. The labors of a lifetime preceded that address, a lifetime devoted to battling for an idea. Four years earlier, in another introductory lecture, Ferri had told his students: "In your life as students and later in your fight for existence in your profession, remember that science and life teach us the lesson to be tolerant with people, because all men of good faith should be respected, whatever may be the philosophy, religion, or political belief they profess; but be inflexible and tenacious defenders of your own ideas. . . . If the idea is wrong, no amount of ability or propaganda will save it from extinction, but if the idea is true, neither academic fear of novelty nor legal persecution can stop its final triumph." And in an address on "human justice" delivered in 1924 in Naples at the Congress for the Advancement of Science, he said: "By temperament I am an idealist because I have always believed—and my life is an example—that life without an ideal, whatever it may be—in art or in science, in politics or in religion—is not worth living."

ENRICO FERRI:
THREE LECTURES GIVEN AT
THE UNIVERSITY OF NAPLES, ITALY
APRIL 22, 23, AND 24, 1901

LECTURE I
[CRITIQUE OF THE
CLASSICAL SCHOOL]

MY Friends:

When, in the turmoil of my daily occupation, I received an invitation, several months ago, from several hundred students of this famous university, to give them a brief summary, in short special lectures, of the principal and fundamental conclusions of criminal sociology, I gladly accepted, because this invitation fell in with two ideals of mine. These two ideals are stirring my heart and are the secret of my life. In the first place, this invitation chimed with the ideal of my personal life, namely, to diffuse and propagate among my brothers the scientific ideas, which my brain has accumulated, not through any merit of mine, but thanks to the lucky prize inherited from my mother in the lottery of life. And the second ideal which this invitation called up before my mind's vision was this: The ideal of young people of Italy, united in morals and intellectual pursuits, feeling in their social lives the glow of a great aim. It would matter little whether this aim would agree with my own ideas or be opposed to them, so long as it should be an ideal which would lift the aspirations of the young people out of the fatal grasp of egoistic interests. Of course, we positivists know very well, that the material requirements of life shape and determine also the moral and intellectual aims of human consciousness. But positive science declares the following to be the indispensable requirement for the regeneration of human ideals: Without an ideal, neither an individual nor a collectivity can live, without it humanity is dead or dying. For it is the fire of an ideal which renders the life of each one of us possible, useful, and fertile. And only by its help can each one of us, in the more or less short course of his or her existence, leave behind traces for the benefit of fellow-beings. The invitation extended to me proves that the students of Naples believe in the inspiring existence of such an ideal of science, and are anxious to learn more about ideas with which the entire world of the present day is occupied, and whose life-giving breath enters even through the windows of the dry courtrooms, when their doors are closed against it.

* * *

Let us now speak of this new science, which has become known in Italy by the name of the Positive School of Criminology. This science, the same as every other phenomenon of scientific evolution, cannot be shortsightedly or conceitedly attributed to the arbitrary initiative of this or that thinker, this or that scientist. We must rather regard it as a natural product, a necessary phenomenon, in the development of that sad and somber department of science which deals with the disease of crime. It is this plague of crime which forms such a gloomy and painful contrast with the splendor of present-day civilization. The nineteenth century has won a great victory over mortality and infectious diseases by means of the masterful progress of physiology and natural science. But while contagious diseases have gradually diminished, we see on the other hand that moral diseases are growing more numerous in our so-called civilization. While typhoid fever, smallpox, cholera, and diphtheria retreated before the remedies which enlightened science applied by means of the experimental method, removing their concrete causes, we see on the other hand that insanity, suicide, and crime, that painful trinity, are growing apace. And this makes it very evident that the science which is principally, if not exclusively, engaged in studying these phenomena of social disease, should feel the necessity of finding a more exact diagnosis of these moral diseases of society, in order to arrive at some effective and more humane remedy, which should more victoriously combat this somber trinity of insanity, suicide, and crime.

The science of positive criminology arose in the last quarter of the nineteenth century as a result of this strange contrast, which would be inexplicable, if we could not discover historical and scientific reasons for its existence. And it is indeed a strange contrast that Italy should have arrived at a perfect theoretical development of a classical school of criminology, while there persists, on the other hand, the disgraceful condition that criminality assumes dimensions never before observed in this country, so that the science of criminology cannot stem the tide of crime in high and low circles. It is for this reason that the positive school of criminology arises out of the very nature of things, the same as every other line of science. It is based on the conditions of our daily life. It would indeed be conceited on our part to claim that we, who are the originators of this new science and its new conclusions, deserve alone the credit for its existence. The brain of the scientist is rather a sort of electrical accumulator, which feels and assimilates the vibrations and heart-beats of life, its splendor and its shame, and derives therefrom the conviction that it must of necessity provide for definite social wants. And on the other hand, it would be an evidence of intellectual shortsightedness on the part of the positivist man of science if he did not recognize the historical accomplishments, which his predecessors in the field of science have left behind as indelible traces of their struggle against the unknown in that brilliant and irksome domain. For this reason, the adherents of the positive school of criminology feel the most sincere reverence for the classic school of criminology. And I am glad today, in accepting the invitation of the students of Naples, to say that this is another reason why their invitation was welcome to me. It is now 16 years since I gave in this same hall a lecture on positive criminology, which was then in its initial stages. It was in 1885, when I had the opportunity to outline the first principles of the positive school of criminology at the invitation of other students, who preceded you on the periodic waves of the intellectual generations. And the renewal of this opportunity gave me so much moral satisfaction that I could not under any circumstances decline your invitation. Then too, the Neapolitan Atheneum has maintained the reputation of the Italian mind in the nineteenth century, also in that science which even foreign scientists admit to be our specialty, namely the science of criminology. In fact, aside from the two terrible books of the Digest,[1] and from the practical criminologists of the Middle Ages who continued the study of criminality, the modern world opened a glorious page in the progress of criminal science with the modest little book of Cesare Beccaria. This progress leads from Cesare Beccaria, by way of Francesco Carrara, to Enrico Pessina.[2]

Enrico Pessina alone remains of the two giants who concluded the cycle of classic school of criminology. In a lucid moment of his scientific consciousness, which soon reverted to the old abstract and metaphysical theories, he announced in an introductory statement in 1879 that criminal justice

1. A casebook of Roman trials and decisions, and one of four parts of the Justinian Code.
2. Enrico Pessina, 1828–1916, Italian jurist, professor, and a leading nineteenth century proponent of the Classical School who came to accept to some extent the naturalistic conception of man and the influence of environment upon the volition of man.

would have to rejuvenate itself in the pure bath of the natural sciences and substitute in place of abstraction the living and concrete study of facts. Naturally every scientist has his function and historical significance; and we cannot expect that a brain which has arrived at the end of its career should turn towards a new direction. At any rate, it is a significant fact that this most renowned representative of the classic school of criminology should have pointed out this need of his special science in this same University of Naples, one year after the inauguration of the positive school of criminology, that he should have looked forward to a time when the study of natural and positive facts would set to rights the old juridical abstractions. And there is still another precedent in the history of this university, which makes scientific propaganda at this place very agreeable for a positivist. It is that six years before that introductory statement by Pessina, Giovanni Bovio[3] gave lectures at this university, which he published later on under the title of *A Critical Study of Criminal Law*. Giovanni Bovio performed in this monograph the function of a critic, but the historical time of his thought prevented him from taking part in the construction of a new science. However, he prepared the ground for new ideas, by pointing out all the rifts and weaknesses of the old building. Bovio maintained that which Gioberti,[4] Ellero,[5] Conforti,[6] Tissot[7] had already maintained, namely that it is impossible to solve the problem which is still the theoretical foundation of the classic school of

3. Giovanni Bovio, 1841–1903, Italian writer, professor, and distinguished legal philosopher noted for his efforts to reconcile the principle of moral liberty of the Classical School and the deterministic position.

4. Vincenzo Gioberti, 1801–1852, Italian ontological philosopher, theologian, and professor.

5. Pietro Ellero, 1833–1933, Italian criminologist, politician, and professor who like Pessina recognized the limitations of the Classical School and contributed to the theoretical foundations of the Positive School.

6. Raffaele Conforti, 1804–1880, Italian politician who built his reputation as a lawyer.

7. Alexandre-Pascal Tissot, 1782–1823, French lawyer and academician who published extensively in the field of jurisprudence.

criminology, the problem of the relation between punishment and crime. No man, no scientist, no legislator, no judge, has ever been able to indicate any absolute standard which would enable us to say that equity demands a definite punishment for a definite crime. We can find some opportunistic expedient, but not a solution of the problem. Of course, if we could decide which is the gravest crime, then we could also decide on the heaviest sentence and formulate a descending scale which would establish the relative fitting proportions between crime and punishment. If it is agreed that patricide is the gravest crime, we mete out the heaviest sentence, death or imprisonment for life, and then we can agree on a descending scale of crime and on a parallel scale of punishments. But the problem begins right with the first stone of the structure, not with the succeeding steps. Which is the greatest penalty proportional to the crime of patricide? Neither science, nor legislation, nor moral consciousness, can offer an absolute standard. Some say: The greatest penalty is death. Others say: No, imprisonment for life. Still others say: Neither death, nor imprisonment for life, but only imprisonment for a time. And if imprisonment for a time is to be the highest penalty, how many years shall it last—thirty, or twenty-five, or ten?

No man can set up any absolute standard in this matter. Giovanni Bovio thus arrived at the conclusion that this internal contradiction in the science of criminology was the inevitable fate of human justice, and that this justice, struggling in the grasp of this internal contradiction, must turn to the civil law and ask for help in its weakness. The same thought had already been illumined by a ray from the bright mind of Filangieri,[8] who died all too soon. And we can derive from this fact the historical rule that the most barbarian

8. Gaetano Filangieri, 1752–1788, Italian politician, scientist, lawyer, and economist who argued that to realize the perfect civil society legislation must consider such enduring, rational, and universal needs as mutual confidence, cooperation and the preservation and security of life. He recommended massive economic, legal, and social reforms—including the estab-

conditions of humanity show a prevalence of a criminal code which punishes without healing; and that the gradual progress of civilization will give rise to the opposite conception of healing without punishing.

Thus it happens that this University of Naples, in which the illustrious representative of the classic school of criminology realized the necessity of its regeneration, and in which Bovio foresaw its sterility, has younger teachers now who keep alive the fire of the positivist tendency in criminal science, such as Penta,[9] Zuccarelli,[10] and others, whom you know. Nevertheless I feel that this faculty of jurisprudence still lacks oxygen in the study of criminal law, because its thought is still influenced by the overwhelming authority of the name of Enrico Pessina. And it is easy to understand that there, where the majestic tree spreads out its branches towards the blue vault, the young plant feels deprived of light and air, while it might have grown strong and beautiful in another place.

The positive school of criminology, then, was born in our own Italy through the singular attraction of the Italian mind toward the study of criminology; and its birth is also due to the peculiar condition of our country with its great and strange contrast between the theoretical doctrines and the painful fact of an ever increasing criminality.

The positive school of criminology was inaugurated by the work of Cesare Lombroso, in 1872. From 1872 to 1876 he opened a new way for the study of criminality by demonstrating in his own person that we must first understand the criminal who offends before we can study and understand

lishment of a class mediatory between the people and the sovereign as well as an active educational effort on the part of the state in promoting virtue.

9. Pasquale Penta, 1859-1904, professor at the University of Naples and noted criminal anthropologist.

10. Angelo Zuccarelli, 1854-1927, professor at the University of Naples, distinguished and widely published criminal anthropologist.

his crime. Lombroso studied the prisoners in the various penitentiaries of Italy from the point of view of anthropology. And he compiled his studies in the reports of the Lombardian Institute of Science and Literature, and published them later together in his work *Criminal Man*. The first edition of this work (1876) remained almost unnoticed, either because its scientific material was meager, or because Cesare Lombroso had not yet drawn any general scientific conclusions, which could have attracted the attention of the world of science and law. But simultaneously with its second edition (1878) there appeared two monographs, which constituted the embryo of the new school, supplementing the anthropological studies of Lombroso with conclusions and systematizations from the point of view of sociology and law. Raffaele Garofalo published in the *Neapolitan Journal of Philosophy and Literature* an essay on criminality, in which he declared that the dangerousness of the criminal was the criterion by which society should measure the function of its defense against the disease of crime. And in the same year, 1878, I took occasion to publish a monograph on the denial of free will and personal responsibility, in which I declared frankly that from now on the science of crime and punishment must look for the fundamental facts of a science of social defense against crime in the human and social life itself. The simultaneous publication of these three monographs caused a stir. The teachers of classic criminology, who had taken kindly to the recommendations of Pessina and Ellero, urging them to study the natural sources of crime, met the new ideas with contempt when the new methods made a determined and radical departure, and became not only the critics, but the zealous opponents of the new theories. And this is easy to understand. For the struggle for existence is an irresistible law of nature, as well for the thousands of germs scattered to the winds by the oak, as for the ideas which grow in the brain of man. But persecutions, calumnies, criticisms, and opposition are powerless against an idea, if it carries within itself the germ of truth. Moreover, we should look upon this phenomenon of a repugnance in the average intellect (whether of the ordinary man or the scientist) for all new ideas as a natural function. For when the brain of some man has felt the light of a new idea, a sneering criticism serves as a touch-stone for it. If the idea is wrong, it will fall by the wayside; if it is right, then criticisms, opposition, and persecution will cull the golden kernel from the unsightly shell, and the idea will march victoriously over everything and everybody. It is so in all walks of life—in art, in politics, in science. Every new idea will rouse against itself naturally and inevitably the opposition of the accustomed thoughts. This is so true that when Cesare Beccaria opened the great historic cycle of the classic school of criminology, he was assaulted by the critics of his time with the same indictments which were brought against us a century later.

When Cesare Beccaria printed his book on crime and penalties in 1764[11] under a false date and place of publication, reflecting the aspirations which gave rise to the impending hurricane of the French revolution; when he hurled himself against all that was barbarian in the mediaeval laws and set loose a storm of enthusiasm among the encyclopedists, and even some of the members of government in France, he was met by a wave of opposition, calumny, and accusation on the part of the majority of jurists, judges, and lights of philosophy. The abbé Facchinei[12] published four volumes against Beccaria, calling him the destroyer of justice and morality, simply because he had combatted the tortures and the death penalty.

11. The 1906 edition printed this date as 1774. While the first edition of Beccaria's *On Crime and Punishments* was published anonymously, there is agreement, however, that the year 1764 is correct.

12. The name Jachinei appears in the 1906 edition. It is apparent that the reference is to Angelo Facchinei, also spelled Fachinei, the Dominican monk whose attack upon Beccaria in 1765 was apparently among the more violent. Maestro, however, refers to Facchinei's writing as a pamphlet and not a four-volume work as suggested by Ferri. See Marcello T. Maestro, *Voltaire and Beccaria as Reformers of Criminal Law* (New York: Columbia University Press, 1942), 63–64.

The tortures, which we incorrectly ascribe to the mental brutality of the judges of those times, were but a logical consequence of the contemporaneous theories. It was felt that in order to condemn a man, one must have the certainty of his guilt, and it was said that the best means of obtaining this certainty, the queen of proofs, was the confession of the criminal. And if the criminal denied his guilt, it was necessary to have recourse to torture, in order to force him to a confession which he withheld from fear of the penalty. The torture soothed, so to say, the conscience of the judge, who was free to condemn as soon as he had obtained a confession. Cesare Beccaria rose with others against the torture. Thereupon the judge and jurists protested that penal justice would be impossible, because it could not get any information, since a man suspected of a crime would not confess his guilt voluntarily. Hence they accused Beccaria of being the protector of robbers and murderers because he wanted to abolish the only means of compelling them to a confession, the torture. But Cesare Beccaria had on his side the magic power of truth. He was truly the electric accumulator of his time, who gathered from its atmosphere the presage of the coming revolution, the stirring of the human conscience. You can find a similar illustration in the works of Daquin[13] in Savoy, of Pinel in France, and of Hack Tuke[14] in England, who strove to bring about a revolution in the treatment of the insane. This episode interests us especially, because it is a perfect illustration of the way traveled by the positive school of criminology. The insane were likewise considered to blame for their insanity. At the dawn of the nineteenth century, the physician Heinroth[15] still wrote that insanity was a moral sin

13. Joseph Daquin, 1733–1815, Italian medical doctor, active in scientific societies. Daquin was a prolific writer who like Pinel argued that the insane should be handled with patience and kindness.
14. The name Hach Take appears in the 1906 edition but the reference is clearly to Daniel Hack Tuke, 1827–1895, English doctor, distinguished and prolific writer on the subject of insanity.
15. The name Hernroth appears in the 1906 edition; however, the refer-

of the insane, because "no one becomes insane, unless he forsakes the straight path of virtue and of the fear of the Lord."

And on this assumption the insane were locked up in horrible dungeons, loaded down with chains, tortured and beaten, for lo! their insanity was their own fault.

At that period, Pinel advanced the revolutionary idea that insanity was not a sin, but a disease like all other diseases. This idea is now commonplace, but in his time it revolutionized the world. It seemed as though this innovation inaugurated by Pinel would overthrow the world and the foundations of society. Well, two years before the storming of the Bastile Pinel walked into the sanitarium of the Salpêtrière and committed the brave act of freeing the insane of the chains that weighed them down. He demonstrated in practice that the insane, when freed of their chains, became quieter, instead of creating wild disorder and destruction. This great revolution of Pinel, Chiarugi,[16] and others changed the attitude of the public mind toward the insane. While formerly insanity had been regarded as a moral sin, the public conscience, thanks to the enlightening work of science, henceforth had to adapt itself to the truth that insanity is a disease like all others, that a man does not become insane because he wants to, but that he becomes insane through hereditary transmission and the influence of the environment in which he lives, being predisposed toward insanity and becoming insane under the pressure of circumstances.

The positive school of criminology accomplished the same revolution in the views concerning the treatment of criminals that the above-named men of science accomplished for the

---

ence is apparently to Johann-Christian-Friedrich-August Heinroth, 1773–1843, distinguished and widely published German physician, physiologist, and professor.

16. Vincenzo Chiarugi, 1759–1820, Italian writer and physician active in initiating more humane methods for treating the insane; known for the reporting of his clinical observations in this area as well as dermatology.

treatment of the insane. The general opinion of classic crim-inalists and of the people at large is that crime involves a moral guilt, because it is due to the free will of the individual who leaves the path of virtue and chooses the path of crime, and therefore it must be suppressed by meeting it with a proportionate quantity of punishment. This is to this day the current conception of crime. And the illusion of a free human will (the only miraculous factor in the eternal ocea of cause and effect) leads to the assumption that one ca choose freely between virtue and vice. How can you stil believe in the existence of a free will, when modern psychology armed with all the instruments of positive modern researc denies that there is any free will and demonstrates that every act of a human being is the result of an interaction between the personality and the environment of man?

And how is it possible to cling to that obsolete idea of moral guilt, according to which every individual is supposed to have the free choice to abandon virtue and give himself up to crime? The positive school of criminology maintains, on the contrary, that it is not the criminal who wills; in order to be a criminal it is rather necessary that the individual should find himself permanently or transitorily in such per-sonal, physical and moral conditions, and live in such an environment, which become for him a chain of cause and effect, externally and internally, that disposes him toward crime. This is our conclusion, which I anticipate, and it con-stitutes the vastly different and opposite method, which the positive school of criminology employs as compared to the leading principle of the classic school of criminal science.

In this method, this essential principle of the positive school of criminology, you will find another reason for the seemingly slow advance of this school. That is very natural. If you consider the great reform carried by the ideas of Cesare Bec-caria into the criminal justice of the Middle Ages, you will see that the great classic school represents but a small step forward, because it leaves the penal justice on the same theoretical and practical basis which it had in the Middle Age and in classic antiquity, that is to say, based on the idea of a moral responsibility of the individual. For Beccaria, for Carrara, for their predecessors, this idea is no more nor less than that mentioned in books 47 and 48 of the Digest: "The criminal is liable to punishment to the extent that he is morally guilty of the crime he has committed." The entire classic school is, therefore, nothing but a series of reforms. Capital punishment has been abolished in some countries, likewise torture, confiscation, corporal punishment. But nevertheless the immense scientific movement of the classic school has remained a mere reform.

It has continued in the nineteenth century to look upon crime in the same way that the Middle Ages did: "Whoever commits murder or theft, is alone the absolute arbiter to decide whether he wants to commit the crime or not." This remains the foundation of the classic school of criminology. This explains why it could travel on its way more rapidly than the positive school of criminology. And yet, it took half a century from the time of Beccaria before the penal codes showed signs of the reformatory influence of the classic school of criminology. So that it has also taken quite a long time to establish it so well that it became accepted by general consent, as it is today. The positive school of criminology was born in 1878, and although it does not stand for a mere reform of the methods of criminal justice, but for a complete and fundamental transformation of criminal justice itself, it has already gone quite a distance and made considerable conquests which begin to show in our country. It is a fact that the penal code now in force in this country represents a compromise, so far as the theory of personal responsibility is concerned, between the old theory of free will and the conclusions of the positive school which denies this free will.

You can find an illustration of this in the eloquent contortions of phantastic logic in the essays on the criminal code written by a great advocate of the classic school of criminology, Mario Pagano,[17] this admirable type of a scientist and patriot, who does not lock himself up in the quiet egoism of his study, but feels the ideal of his time stirring within him and gives up his life to it. He has written three lines of a simple nudity that reveals much, in which he says: "A man is responsible for the crimes which he commits; if, in committing a crime, his will is half free, he is responsible to the extent of one-half; if one-third, he is responsible one-third." There you have the uncompromising and absolute classic theorem. But in the penal code of 1890, you will find that the famous article 45 intends to base the responsibility for a crime on the simple will, to the exclusion of the free will. However, the Italian judge has continued to base the exercise of penal justice on the supposed existence of the free will, and pretends not to know that the number of scientists denying the free will is growing. Now, how is it possible that so terrible an office as that of sentencing criminals retains its stability or vacillates, according to whether the first who denies the existence of a free will deprives this function of its foundation?

Truly, it is said that this question has been too difficult for the new Italian penal code. And, for this reason, it was thought best to base the responsibility for a crime on the idea that a man is guilty simply for the reason that he wanted to commit the crime; and that he is not responsible if he did not want to commit it. But this is an eclectic way out of the difficulty, which settles nothing, for in the same code we have the rule that involuntary criminals are also punished, so that involuntary killing and wounding are punished with imprisonment the same as voluntary deeds of this kind. We have heard it said in such cases that the result may not have been intended, but the action bringing it about was. If a hunter shoots through a hedge and kills or wounds a person, he did not intend to

17. Francesco Mario Pagano, 1748–1799, Italian jurist, professor of penal law at the University of Naples who sought a reconciliation between the views of Rousseau and Vico.

kill, and yet he is held responsible because his first act, the shooting, was voluntary.

That statement applies to involuntary crimes, which are committed by some positive act. But what about involuntary crimes of omission? In a railway station, where the movements of trains represent the daily whirl of traffic in men, things, and ideas, every switch is a delicate instrument which may cause a derailment. The railway management places a switchman on duty at this delicate post. But in a moment of fatigue, or because he had to work inhumanly long hours of work, which exhausted all his nervous elasticity, or for other reasons, the switchman forgets to set the switch and causes a railroad accident, in which people are killed and wounded. Can it be said that he intended the first act? Assuredly not, for he did not intend anything and did not do anything. The hunter who fires a shot has at least had the intention of shooting. But the switchman did not want to forget (for in that case he would be indirectly to blame); he has simply forgotten from sheer fatigue to do his duty; he has had no intention whatever, and yet you hold him responsible in spite of all that! The fundamental logic of your reasoning in this case corresponds to the logic of the things. Does it not happen every day in the administration of justice that the judges forget about the neutral expedient of the legislator who devised this relative progress of the penal code, which pretends to base the responsibility of a man on the neutral and naive criterion of a will without freedom of will? Do they not follow their old mental habits in the administration of justice and apply the obsolete criterion of the free will, which the legislator thought fit to abandon? We see, then, as a result of this imperfect and insincere innovation in penal legislation this flagrant contradiction, that the magistrates assume the existence of a free will, while the legislator has decided that it shall not be assumed. Now, in science as well as in legislation, we should follow a direct and logical line, such as that of the classic school or the positive school of criminology. But whoever thinks he has solved a problem when he gives us a solution which is neither fish nor fowl, comes to the most absurd and iniquitous conclusions. You see what happens every day. If to-morrow some beastly and incomprehensible crime is committed, the conscience of the judge is troubled by this question: Was the person who committed this crime morally free to act or not? He may also invoke the help of legislation, and he may take refuge in article 46,* or in that compromise of article 47,† which admits a responsibility of one-half or one-third, and he would decide on a penalty of one-half or one-third.

All this may take place in the case of a grave and strange crime. And on the other hand, go to the municipal courts or to the police courts, where the magic lantern of justice throws its rays upon the nameless human beings who have stolen a bundle of wood in a hard winter, or who have slapped some one in the face during a brawl in a saloon. And if they should find a defending lawyer who would demand the appointment of a medical expert, watch the recep-

* Article 46: "A person is not subject to punishment, if at the moment of his deed he was in a mental condition which deprived him of consciousness or of the freedom of action. But if the judge considers it dangerous to acquit the prisoner, he has to transfer him to the care of the proper authorities, who will take the necessary precautions." (Note appears in 1906 edition.)

† Article 47: "If the mental condition mentioned in the foregoing article was such as to considerably decrease the responsibility, without eliminating it entirely, the penalty fixed upon the crime committed is reduced according to the following rules:

"I. In place of penitentiary, imprisonment for not less than six years.

"II. In place of the permanent loss of civic rights, a loss of these rights for a stipulated time.

"III. Whenever it is a question of a penalty of more than twelve years, it is reduced to from three to ten years; if of more than six years, but not more than twelve, it is reduced to from one to five years; in other cases, the reduction is to be one-half of the ordinary penalty.

"IV. A fine is reduced to one-half.

"V. If the penalty would be a restriction of personal liberty, the judge may order the prisoner to a workhouse, until the proper authorities object, when the remainder of the sentence is carried out in the usual manner." (Note appears in 1906 edition.)

58

tion he would get from the judge. When justice is surprised by a beastly and strange crime, it feels the entire foundation of its premises shaking, it halts for a moment, it calls in the help of legal medicine, and reflects before it sentences. But in the case of those poor nameless creatures, justice does not stop to consider whether that microbe in the criminal world who steals under the influence of hereditary or acquired degeneration, or in the delirium of chronic hunger, is not worthy of more pity. It rather replies with a mephistophelian grin when he begs for a humane understanding of his case.

It is true that there is now and then in those halls of justice, which remain all too frequently closed to the living wave of public sentiment, some more intelligent and serene judge who is touched by this painful understanding of the actual human life. Then he may, under the illogical conditions of penal justice, with its compromise between the exactness of the classic and that of the positive school of criminology, seek for some expedient which may restore him to equanimity.

In 1832, France introduced a penal innovation, which seemed to represent an advance on the field of justice, but which is in reality a denial of justice: The expedient of *extenuating circumstances*. The judge does not ask for the advice of the court physician in the case of some forlorn criminal, but condemns him without a word of rebuke to society for its complicity. But in order to assuage his own conscience he grants him extenuating circumstances, which seem a concession of justice, but are, in reality, a denial of justice. For you either believe that a man is responsible for his crime, and in that case the concession of extenuating circumstances is a hypocrisy; or you grant them in good faith, and then you admit that the man was in circumstances which reduced his moral responsibility, and thereby the extenuating circumstances become a denial of justice. For if your conviction concerning such circumstances were sincere, you would go to the bottom of them and examine with the light of your understanding all those innumerable conditions which contribute toward those extenuating circumstances. But what are those extenuating circumstances? Family conditions? Take it that a child is left alone by its parents, who are swallowed up in the whirl of modern industry, which overthrows the laws of nature and forbids the necessary rest, because steam engines do not get tired and day work must be followed by night work, so that the setting of the sun is no longer the signal for the laborer to rest, but to begin a new shift of work. Take it that this applies not alone to adults, but also to human beings in the growing stage, whose muscular power may yield some profit for the capitalists. Take it that even the mother, during the period of sacred maternity, becomes a cog in the machinery of industry. And you will understand that the child must grow up, left to its own resources, in the filth of life, and that its history will be inscribed in criminal statistics, which are the shame of our so-called civilization.

Of course, in this first lecture I cannot give you even a glimpse of the positive results of that modern science which has studied the criminal and his environment instead of his crimes. And I must, therefore, limit myself to a few hints concerning the historical origin of the positive school of criminology. I ought to tell you something concerning the question of free will. But you will understand that such a momentous question, which is worthy of a deep study of the many-sided physical, moral, intellectual life, cannot be summed up in a few short words. I can only say that the tendency of modern natural sciences, in physiology as well as psychology, has overruled the illusions of those who would fain persist in watching psychological phenomena merely within themselves and think that they can understand them without any other means. On the contrary, positive science, backed by the testimony of anthropology and of the study of the environment, has arrived at the following conclusions: The admission of a free will is out of the question. For if the free will is but an illusion of our internal being, it is not a real faculty possessed by the human mind. Free will would imply that the human will, confronted by the choice of making voluntarily a certain determination, has the last decisive word under the pressure of circumstances contending for and against this decision; that it is free to decide for or against a certain course independently of internal and external circumstances, which play upon it, according to the laws of cause and effect.

Take it that a man has insulted me. I leave the place in which I have been insulted, and with me goes the suggestion of forgiveness or of murder and vengeance. And then it is assumed that a man has his complete free will, unless he is influenced by circumstances explicitly enumerated by the law, such as minority, congenital deaf-muteness, insanity, habitual drunkenness, and, to a certain extent, violent passion. If a man is not in a condition mentioned in this list, he is considered in possession of his free will, and if he murders he is held morally responsible and therefore punished.

This illusion of a free will has its source in our inner consciousness, and is due solely to the ignorance in which we find ourselves concerning the various motives and different external and internal conditions which press upon our mind at the moment of decision.

If a man knows the principal causes which determine a certain phenomenon, he says that this phenomenon is inevitable. If he does not know them, he considers it as an accident, and this corresponds in the physical field to the arbitrary phenomenon of the human will which does not know whether it shall decide this way or that. For instance, some of us were of the opinion, and many still are, that the coming and going of meteorological phenomena was accidental and could not be foreseen. But in the meantime, science has demonstrated that they are likewise subject to the law of causality, because it discovered the causes which enable us to foresee their course. Thus weather prognosis has made wonderful progress by the help of a network of telegraphically connected meteorological stations, which succeeded in demonstrating the connection between cause and effect in the case of hurricanes, as

well as of any other physical phenomenon. It is evident that
the idea of accident, applied to physical nature, is unscientific.
Every physical phenomenon is the necessary effect of the
causes that determined it beforehand. If those causes are known
to us, we have the conviction that that phenomenon is necessary, is fate, and, if we do not know them, we think it is
accidental. The same is true of human phenomena. But since
we do not know the internal and external causes in the majority of cases, we pretend that they are free pheonomena,
that is to say, that they are not determined necessarily by
their causes. Hence the spiritualistic conception of the free
will implies that every human being, in spite of the fact that
their internal and external conditions are necessarily predeter-
mined, should be able to come to a deliberate decision by the
mere fiat of his or her free will, so that, even though the sum
of all the causes demands a no, he or she can decide in favor
of yes, and vice versa. Now, who is there that thinks, when
deliberating some action, what are the causes that determine
his choice? We can justly say that the greater part of our
actions are determined by habit, that we make up our minds
almost from custom, without considering the reason for or
against. When we get up in the morning we go about our
customary business quite automatically, we perform it as a
function in which we do not think of a free will. We think
of that only in unusual and grave cases, when we are called
upon to make some special choice, the so-called voluntary
deliberation, and then we weigh the reasons for or against;
we ponder, we hesitate what to do. Well, even in such cases,
so little depends on our will in the deliberations which we
are about to take that if any one were to ask us one minute
before we have decided what we are going to do, we should
not know what we were going to decide. So long as we are
undecided, we cannot foresee what we are going to decide;
for under the conditions in which we live that part of the
psychic process takes place outside of our consciousness. And
since we do not know its causes, we cannot tell what will be

its effects. Only after we have come to a certain decision can we imagine that it was due to our voluntary action. But shortly before we could not tell, and that proves that it did not depend on us alone. Suppose, for instance, that you have decided to play a joke on a fellow-student, and that you carry it out. He takes it unkindly. You are surprised, because that is contrary to his habits and your expectations. But after a while you learn that your friend had received bad news from home on the preceding morning and was therefore not in a condition to feel like joking, and then you say: "If we had known that we should not have decided to spring the joke on him." That is equivalent to saying that, if the balance of your will had been inclined toward the deciding motive of no, you would have decided no; but not knowing that your friend was distressed and not in his habitual frame of mind, you decided in favor of yes. This sentence: "If I had known this I should not have done that" is an outcry of our internal consciousness, which denies the existence of a free will.

On the other hand, nothing is created and nothing destroyed either in matter or in force, because both matter and force are eternal and indestructible. They transform themselves in the most diversified manner, but not an atom is added or taken away, not one vibration more or less takes place. And so it is the force of external and internal circumstances which determines the decision of our will at any given moment. The idea of a free will, however, is a denial of the law of cause and effect, both in the field of philosophy and theology. Saint Augustine and Martin Luther furnish irrefutable theological arguments for the denial of a free will. The omnipotence of God is irreconcilable with the idea of free will. If everything that happens does so because a superhuman and omnipotent power wants it (*Not a single leaf falls to the ground without the will of God*), how can a son murder his father without the permission and will of God? For this reason Saint Augustine and Martin Luther have written *de servo arbitrio*.[18]

18. The enslaved will.

But since theological arguments serve only those who believe in the concept of a god, which is not given to us by science, we take recourse to the laws which we observe in force and matter, and to the law of causality. If modern science has discovered the universal link which connects all phenomena through cause and effect, which shows that every phenomenon is the result of causes which have preceded it: if this is the law of causality, which is at the very bottom of modern scientific thought, then it is evident that the admission of free thought is equivalent to an overthrow of this law, according to which every effort is proportionate to its cause. In that case, this law, which reigns supreme in the entire universe, would dissolve itself into naught at the feet of the human being, who would create effects with his free will not corresponding to their causes! It was all right to think so at a time when people had an entirely different idea of human beings. But the work of modern science, and its effect on practical life, has resulted in tracing the relations of each one of us with the world and with our fellow beings. And the influence of science may be seen in the elimination of great illusions which in former centuries swayed this or that part of civilized humanity. The scientific thought of Copernicus and Galilei[19] did away with the illusions which led people to believe that the earth was the center of the universe and of creation.

Take Cicero's book *de Officiis*, or the *Divina Commedia* of Dante, and you will find that to them the earth is the center of creation, that the infinite stars circle around it, and that man is the king of animals: a geocentric and anthropocentric illusion inspired by immeasurable conceit. But Copernicus and Galilei came and demonstrated that the earth does not stand still, but that it is a grain of cosmic matter hurled into blue infinity and rotating since time unknown around its central body, the sun, which originated from an immense

19. Ferri consistently refers to Galileo Galilei by his surname—an uncommon practice today.

primitive nebula. Galilei was subjected to tortures by those who realized that this new theory struck down many a religious legend and many a moral creed. But Galilei had spoken the truth, and nowadays humanity no longer indulges in the illusion that the earth is the center of creation.

But men live on illusions and give way but reluctantly to the progress of science, in order to devote themselves arduously to the ideal of the new truths which rise out of the essence of things of which mankind is a part. After the geocentric illusion had been destroyed, the anthropocentric illusion still remained. On earth, man was still supposed to be king of creation, the center of terrestrial life. All species of animals, plants, and minerals were supposed to be created expressly for him, and to have had from time immemorial the forms which we see now, so that the fauna and flora living on our planet have always been what they are today. And Cicero, for instance, said that the heavens were placed around the earth and man in order that he might admire the beauty of the starry firmament at night, and that animals and plants were created for his use and pleasure. But in 1856 Charles Darwin came and, summarizing the results of studies that had been carried on for a century, destroyed in the name of science the superb illusion that man is the king and center of creation. He demonstrated, amid the attacks and calumnies of the lovers of darkness, that man is not the king of creation, but merely the last link of the zoological chain, that nature is endowed with eternal energies by which animal and plant life, the same as mineral life (for even in crystals the laws of life are at work), are transformed from the invisible microbe to the highest form, man.

The anthropocentric illusion rebelled against the word of Darwin, accusing him of lowering the human life to the level of the dirt or of the brute. But a disciple of Darwin gave the right answer, while propagating the Darwinian theory at the University of Jena. It was Haeckel, who concluded: "For my part, and so far as my human consciousness is concerned,

I prefer to be an immensely perfected ape rather than to be a degenerated and debased Adam."

Gradually the anthropocentric illusion has been compelled to give way before the results of science, and today the theories of Darwin have become established among our ideas. But another illusion still remains, and science, working in the name of reality, will gradually eliminate it, namely the illusion that the nineteenth century has established a permanent order of society. While the geocentric and anthropocentric illusions have been dispelled, the illusion of the immobility and eternity of classes still persists. But it is well to remember that in Holland in the sixteenth century, in England in the seventeenth, in Europe since the revolution of 1789, we have seen that freedom of thought in science, literature, and art, for which the bourgeoisie fought, triumphed over the tyranny of the mediaeval dogma. And this condition, instead of being a glorious but transitory stage, is supposed to be the end of the development of humanity, which is henceforth condemned not to perfect itself any more by further changes. This is the illusion which serves as a fundamental argument against the positive school of criminology, since it is claimed that a penal justice enthroned on the foundations of Beccaria and Carrara would be a revolutionary heresy. It is also this illusion which serves as an argument against those who draw the logical consequences in regard to the socialistic future of humanity, for the science which takes its departure from the work of Copernicus, Galilei, and Darwin arrives logically at socialism. Socialism is but the natural and physical transformation of the economic and social institutions. Of course, so long as the geocentric and anthropocentric illusions dominate, it is natural that the love of stability should impress itself upon science and life. How could this living atom, which the human being is, undertake to change that order of creation, which makes of the earth the center of the universe and of man the center of life? Not until science had introduced the conception of a natural formation and transformation of the solar system, as well as of the fauna and flora, did the human mind grasp the idea that thought and action can transform the world.

For this reason we believe that the study of the criminal, and the logical consequences therefrom, will bring about the complete transformation of human justice, not only as a theory laid down in scientific books, but also as a practical function applied every day to that living and suffering portion of humanity which has fallen into crime. We have the undaunted faith that the work of scientific truth will transform penal justice into a simple function of preserving society from the disease of crime, divested of all relics of vengeance, hatred, and punishment, which still survive in our day as living reminders of the barbarian stage. We still hear the "public vengeance" invoked against the criminal today, and justice has still for its symbol a sword, which it uses more than the scales. But a judge born of a woman cannot weigh the moral responsibility of one who has committed murder or theft. Not until the experimental and scientific method shall look for the causes of that dangerous malady, which we call crime, in the physical and psychic organism, and in the family and the environment, of the criminal, will justice guided by science discard the sword which now descends bloody upon those poor fellow-beings who have fallen victims to crime, and become a clinical function, whose prime object shall be to remove or lessen in society and individuals the causes which incite to crime. Then alone will justice refrain from wreaking vengeance, after a crime has been committed, with the shame of an execution or the absurdity of solitary confinement.

On the one hand, human life depends on the word of a judge, who may err in the case of capital punishment; and society cannot end the life of a man, unless the necessity of legitimate self-defense demands it. On the other hand, solitary confinement came in with the second current of the classic school of criminology, when at the same time, in which Beccaria promulgated his ideas, John Howard traveled all over

Europe describing the unmentionable horrors of mass imprisonment, which became a center of infection for society at large. Then the classic school went to the other extreme of solitary confinement, after the model of America, whence we adopted the systems of Philadelphia and Harrisburg[20] in the first half of the nineteenth century. Isolation for the night is also our demand, but we object to continuous solitary confinement by day and night. Pasquale Mancini[21] called solitary confinement "a living grave," in order to reassure the timorous, when in the name of the classic school, whose valiant champion he was, he demanded in 1876 the abolition of capital punishment. Yet in his swan song he recognized that the future would belong to the positive school of criminology. And it is this "living grave" against which we protest. It cannot possibly be an act of human justice to bury a human being in a narrow cell, within four walls, to prevent this being from having any contact with social life, and to say to him at the end of his term: Now that your lungs are no longer accustomed to breathing the open air, now that your legs are no longer used to the rough roads, go, but take care not to have a relapse, or your sentence will be twice as hard.

In reality, solitary confinement makes of a human being either a stupid creature, or a raving beast. And *s'io dico il vero, l'effeto nol nasconde*—if I speak the truth, the facts

20. The extreme of the solitary confinement system in the United States was the Pennsylvania system, which required isolation at all times. Ferri's reference is probably to Pittsburgh (not Harrisburg) and the Western Penitentiary which opened in 1826. The Western Penitentiary and the Eastern Penitentiary at Philadelphia were both based on the Pennsylvania system. In terms of the rationale sustaining them they are not typically thought of as separate systems.

21. Pasquale Stanislao Mancini, 1817–1888, Italian jurist, professor of law, prolific writer; served as minister of several departments; a liberal, anti-cleric, and leader in the opposition to capital punishment. Noted for his view that the system of justice must be combined with social utility and that punishment must not only provide for expiation but must also prevent crime. See Lecture III, note 1.

will also reveal it—for criminality increases and expands, honest people remain unprotected, and those who are struck by the law do not improve, but become ever more antisocial through the repeated relapses. And so we have that contrast which I mentioned in the beginning of my lecture, that the theoretical side of criminal science is so perfected, while criminal conditions are painfully in evidence. The inevitable conclusion is the necessity of a progressive transformation of the science of crime and punishment.

LECTURE II
[CAUSES OF
CRIMINAL BEHAVIOR]

W E saw yesterday in a short historical review that the classic cycle of the science of crime and punishment, originated by Cesare Baccaria more than a century ago, was followed in our country, some twenty years since, by the scientific movement of the positive school of criminology. Let us see today how this school studied the problem of criminality, reserving for tomorrow the discussion of the remedies proposed by this school for the disease of criminality.

When a crime is committed in some place, attracting public attention either through the atrocity of the case or the strangeness of the criminal deed—for instance, one that is not connected with bloodshed, but with intellectual fraud—there are at once two tendencies that make themselves felt in the public conscience. One of them, pervading the overwhelming majority of individual consciences, asks: How is this? What for? Why did that man commit such a crime? This question is asked by everybody and occupies mostly the attention of those who do not look upon the case from the point of view of cirminology. On the other hand, those who occupy themselves with criminal law represent the other tendency, which manifests itself when acquainted with the news of this crime. This is a limited portion of the public conscience, which tries to study the problem from the standpoint of the technical jurist. The lawyers, the judges, the officials of the police, ask themselves: What is the name of the crime committed by that man under such circumstances? Must it be classed as murder or patricide, attempted or incompleted manslaughter, and, if directed against property, is it theft, or illegal appropriation, or fraud? And the entire apparatus of practical criminal justice forgets at once the first problem, which occupies the majority of the public conscience, the question of the causes that led to this crime, in order to devote itself exclusively to the technical side of the problem, which constitutes the juridical anatomy of the inhuman and antisocial deed perpetrated by the criminal.

In these two tendencies you have a photographic reproduction of the two schools of criminology. The classic school, which looks upon the crime as a juridical problem, occupies itself with its name, its definition, its juridical analysis, leaves the personality of the criminal in the background and remembers it only so far as exceptional circumstances explicitly stated in the law books refer to it: whether he is a minor, a deaf-mute, whether it is a case of insanity, whether he was drunk at the time the crime was committed. Only in these strictly defined cases does the classic school occupy itself theoretically with the personality of the criminal. But ninety times in one hundred these exceptional circumstances do not exist or cannot be shown to exist, and penal justice limits itself to the technical definition of the fact. But when the case comes up in the criminal court, or before the jurors, practice demonstrates that there is seldom a discussion between the lawyers of the defense and the judges for the purpose of ascertaining the most exact definition of the fact, of determining whether it is a case of attempted or merely projected crime, of finding out whether there are any of the juridical elements defined in this or that article of the code. The judge is rather face to face with the problem of ascertaining why, under what conditions, for what reasons, the man has committed the crime. This is the supreme and simple human problem. But hitherto it has been left to a more or less perspicacious, more or less gifted, empiricism, and there have been no scientific standards, no methodical collection of facts, no observations and conclusions, save those of the positive school of criminology. This school alone makes an attempt to solve in every case of crime the problem of its natural origin, of the reasons and conditions that induced a man to commit such and such a crime.

For instance, about 3,000 cases of manslaughter are registered every year in Italy. Now, open any work inspired by the classic school of criminology, and ask the author why 3,000 men are the victims of manslaughter every year in Italy, and how it is that there are not sometimes only as many as, say, 300 cases, the number committed in England, which has nearly the same number of inhabitants as Italy; and how it is that there are not sometimes 300,000 such cases in Italy instead of 3,000?

It is useless to open any work of classical criminology for this purpose, for you will not find an answer to these questions in them. No one, from Beccaria to Carrara, has ever thought of this problem, and they could not have asked it, considering their point of departure and their method. In fact, the classic criminologists accept the phenomenon of criminality as an accomplished fact. They analyze it from the point of view of the technical jurist, without asking how this criminal fact may have been produced, and why it repeats itself in greater or smaller numbers from year to year, in every country. The theory of a free will, which is their foundation, excludes the possibility of this scientific question, for according to it the crime is the product of the fiat of the human will. And if that is admitted as a fact, there is nothing left to account for. The manslaughter was committed, because the criminal wanted to commit it; and that is all there is to it. Once the theory of a free will is accepted as a fact, the deed depends on the fiat, the voluntary determination, of the criminal, and all is said.

But if, on the other hand, the positive school of criminology denies, on the ground of researches in scientific physiological psychology, that the human will is free and does not admit that one is a criminal because he wants to be, but declares that a man commits this or that crime only when he lives in definitely determined conditions of personality and environment which induce him necessarily to act in a certain way, then alone does the problem of the origin of criminality begin to be submitted to a preliminary analysis, and then alone does criminal law step out of the narrow and arid limits of technical jurisprudence and become a true social and human science in the highest and noblest meaning of the word. It is vain to insist with such stubbornness as that of the classic school of criminology on juristic formulae by which the distinction between illegal appropriation and theft, between fraud and other forms of crime against property, and so forth, is determined, when this method does not give to society one single word which would throw light upon the reasons that make a man a criminal and upon the efficacious remedy by which society could protect itself against criminality.

It is true that the classic school of criminology has likewise its remedy against crime—namely, punishment. But this is the only remedy of that school, and in all the legislation inspired by the theories of that school in all the countries of the civilized world there is no other remedy against crime but repression.

But Bentham has said: Every time that punishment is inflicted it proves its inefficacy, for it did not prevent the committal of that crime. Therefore, this remedy is worthless. And a deeper study of the cause of crime demonstrates that if a man does not commit a certain crime, this is due to entirely different reasons than a fear of the penalty, very strong and fundamental reasons which are not to be found in the threats of legislators.

73

These threats, if nevertheless carried out by police and prison keepers, run counter to those conditions. A man who intends to commit a crime, or who is carried away by a violent passion, by a psychological hurricane which drowns his moral sense, is not checked by threats of punishment, because the volcanic eruption of passion prevents him from reflecting. Or he may decide to commit a crime after due premeditation and preparation, and in that case the penalty is powerless to check him, because he hopes to escape with impunity. All criminals will tell you unanimously that the only thing which impelled them when they were deliberating a crime was the expectation that they would go scot free. If they had had the least suspicion that they might be detected and punished they would not have committed the crime. The only exception is the case in which a crime is the result of a mental explosion caused by a violent outburst of passion. And if you wish to have a very convincing illustration of the psychological inefficacy of legal threats, you have but to think of that curious crime which has now assumed a frequency never known to former centuries, namely the making of counterfeit money. For since paper money—from want or for reasons of expediency—has become a substitute of metal coin in the civilized countries, the making of counterfeit paper money has become very frequent in the nineteenth century. Now a counterfeiter, in committing his crime, must compel his mind to imitate closely the inscription of the bill, letter for letter, including that threatening passage, which says: "The law punishes counterfeiting . . .," etc. Can you see before your mind's eye a counterfeiter, in the act of engraving on the stone or the plate these words: "The law punishes counterfeiting . . ."? Others may ignore the penalty that awaits them, but he cannot. This illustration is convincing, for in cases of other crimes one may always assume that the criminal acted without thinking of the future, even when he was not in a transport of passion. But in the case of the counterfeiter the very act of committing the crime reminds him of the threat of the law, and yet he is imperturbable while perpetrating it.

74

Crime has its natural causes, which lie outside of that mathematical point called the free will of the criminal. Aside from being a juridical phenomenon, which it would be well to examine by itself, every crime is above all a natural and social phenomenon, and should be studied primarily as such. We need not go through so hard a course of study merely for the purpose of walking over the razor edge of juristic definitions and to find out, for instance, that from the time Romagnosi[1] made a distinction between incompleted and attempted crime rivers of ink have been spilled in the attempt to find the distinguishing elements of these two degrees of crime. And finally, when the German legislator concluded to make no distinction between incompleted and attempted crime and to recognize only the completed crime in his code of 1871, we witnessed the spectacle of Carrara praising that legislator for leaving that subtle distinction out of his code. A strange conclusion on the part of a science, which cudgels its brains for a century to find the marks of distinction between attempted and incompleted crime, and then praises the legislator for ignoring it. And another classic jurist, Buccellati,[2] proposed to do away with the theory of attempted crime by simply defining it as a crime by itself, or as— a violation of police laws! A science which comes to such conclusions is a science which moves in metaphysical abstractions, and we shall see that all these finespun questions which abound in classical science lose all practical value before the necessity of saving society from the plague of crime.

The method which we, on the other hand, have inaugurated is the following: Before we study crime from the point of view of a juristic phenomenon, we must study the causes to which the annual recurrence of crimes in all countries is due. These are natural causes, which I have classified under the three heads

1. Giovanni Romagnosi, 1761–1835, Italian lawyer, judge, criminologist, and professor of law who stressed the need for indirect preventive measures to deal with crime.

2. The reference is apparently to Father Antonio Buccellati, 1831–1890, Italian lawyer, professor of ecclesiastic and penal law, and an architect of Italian penal law.

of anthropological, telluric, and social. Every crime, from the smallest to the most atrocious, is the result of the interaction of these three causes, the anthropological condition of the criminal, the telluric environment in which he is living, and the social environment in which he is born, living, and operating. It is a vain beginning to separate the meshes of this net of criminality. There are still those who would maintain the one-sided standpoint that the origin of crime may be traced to only one of these elements, for instance, to the social element alone. So far as I am concerned, I have combatted this opinion from the very inauguration of the positive school of criminology, and I combat it today. It is certainly easy enough to think that the entire origin of all crime is due to the unfavorable social conditions in which the criminal lives. But an objective, method-ical, observation demonstrates that social conditions alone do not suffice to explain the origin of criminality, although it is true that the prevalence of the influence of social conditions is an incontestable fact in the case of the greater number of crimes, especially of the lesser ones. But there are crimes which cannot be explained by the influence of social conditions alone. If you regard the general condition of misery as the sole source of criminality, then you cannot get around the difficulty that out of one thousand individuals living in misery from the day of their birth to that of their death only one hundred or two hundred become criminals, while the other nine hundred or eight hundred either sink into biological weakness, or become harmless maniacs, or commit suicide without perpetrating any crime. If poverty were the sole determining cause, one thousand out of one thousand poor ought to become criminals. If only two hundred become criminals, while one hundred commit suicide, one hundred end as maniacs, and the other six hundred remain honest in their social condition, then poverty alone is not sufficient to explain criminality. We must add the anthropo-logical and telluric factor. Only by means of these three ele-ments of natural influence can criminality be explained. Of course, the influence of either the anthropological or telluric or social element varies from case to case. If you have a case of simple theft, you may have a far greater influence of the social factor than of the anthropological factor. On the other hand, if you have a case of murder, the anthropological element will have a far greater influence than the social. And so on in every case of crime, and every individual that you will have to judge on the bench of the criminal.

The anthropological factor. It is precisely here that the genius of Cesare Lombroso established a new science, because in his search after the causes of crime he studied the anthropological condition of the criminal. This condition concerns not only the organic and anatomical constitution, but also the psychological, it represents the organic and psychological personality of the criminal. Every one of us inherits at birth, and personifies in life, a certain organic and psychological combination. This constitutes the individual factor of human activity, which either remains normal through life, or becomes criminal or insane. The anthropological factor, then, must not be restricted, as some laymen would restrict it, to the study of the form of the skull or the bones of the criminal. Lombroso had to begin his studies with the anatomical conditions of the criminal, because the skulls may be studied most easily in the museums. But he continued by also studying the brain and the other physiological conditions of the individual, the state of sensibility, and the circulation of matter. And this entire series of studies is but a necessary scientific introduction to the study of the psychology of the criminal, which is precisely the one problem that is of direct and immediate importance. It is this problem which the lawyer and the public prosecutor should solve before discussing the juridical aspect of any crime, for this reveals the causes which induced the criminal to commit a crime. At present there is no methodical standard for a psychological investigation, although such an investigation was introduced into the scope of classic penal law. But for this reason the results of the positive school penetrate into the lecture rooms of the universities of jurisprudence, whenever a law is required for the judicial arraignment of the criminal as a living and feeling human being. And even though the positive school is not mentioned, all profess to be studying the material furnished by it, for instance, its analyses of the sentiments of the criminal, his moral sense, his behavior before, during, and after the criminal act, the presence of remorse which people, judging the criminal after their own feelings, always suppose the criminal to feel, while, in fact, it is seldom present. This is the anthropological factor, which may assume a pathological form, in which case articles 46 and 47 of the penal code remember that there is such a thing as the personality of the criminal. However, aside from insanity, there are thousands of other organic and psychological conditions of the personality of criminals, which a judge might perhaps lump together under the name of extenuating circumstances, but which science desires to have thoroughly investigated. This is not done today, and for this reason the idea of extenuating circumstances constitutes a denial of justice.

This same anthropological factor also includes that which each one of us has: the race character. Nowadays the influence of race on the destinies of peoples and persons is much discussed in sociology, and there are one-sided schools that pretend to solve the problems of history and society by means of that racial influence alone, to which they attribute an absolute importance. But while there are some who maintain that the history of peoples is nothing but the exclusive product of racial character, there are others who insist that the social conditions of peoples and individuals are alone determining. The one is as much a one-sided and incomplete theory as the other. The study of collective society or of the single individual has resulted in the understanding that the life of society and of the individual is always the product of the inextricable net of the anthropological, telluric, and social elements. Hence the influence of the race cannot be ignored in the study of nations and personalities, although it is not the exclusive factor which would suffice to explain the criminality of a nation or an individual. Study, for instance, manslaughter in Italy, and, although you will find it difficult to isolate one of the factors of criminality from the network of the other circumstances and conditions that produce it, yet there are such eloquent instances of the influence of racial character, that it would be like denying the existence of daylight if one tried to ignore the influence of the ethnical factor on criminality.

In Italy there are two currents of criminality, two tendencies which are almost diametrically opposed to one another. The crimes due to hot blood and muscle grow in intensity from northern to southern Italy, while the crimes against property increase from south to north. In northern Italy, where movable property is more developed, the crime of theft assumes a greater intensity, while crimes due to conditions of the blood are decreasing on account of the lesser poverty and the resulting lesser degeneration of the people. In the south, on the other hand, crimes against property are less frequent and crimes of blood more frequent. Still there also are in southern Italy certain cases where criminality of the blood is less frequent, and you cannot explain this in any other way than by the influence of racial character. If you take a geographical map of manslaughter in Italy, you will see that from the minimum, from Lombardy, Piedmont, and Venice, the intensity increases until it reaches its maximum in the insular and peninsular extreme of the south. But even there you will find certain cases in which manslaughter shows a lesser intensity.

For instance, the province of Benevent is surrounded by other provinces which show a maximum of crimes due to conditions of blood, while it registers a smaller number. Naples, again, shows a considerably smaller number of such cases than the provinces surrounding it, but it has a greater number of unpremeditated cases of manslaughter. Messina, Catania, and Syracuse have a remarkably smaller number of blood crimes than Trapani, Girgenti, and Palermo. It has been attempted to claim that this difference in criminality is due to social conditions, because the agricultural conditions in eastern Sicily are less degrading than those of Girgenti and Trapani, where the sulphur mines compel the miners to live miserably. But we should like to ask the following question in opposition to this idea: Why and in what respect are the agricultural conditions in some provinces better than in others? This condition is merely itself a result, not a cause of the first degree.

Since the theory of historical materialism, which I prefer to call economic determinism, has demonstrated that political, moral, and intellectual phenomena are reactions on the economic conditions of any time and place, the attempt has been made to interpret this theory very narrowly and to pretend that the economic condition of a nation is a primary cause and not determined by any other. For my part, ever since I have demonstrated the perfect accord between the Marxian and the Darwinian theories, I have said: Very well, the economic conditions of a nation explain its political, moral, intellectual conditions, but the economic condition is in its turn the result of other factors. For instance, how can the industrialism of England in the nineteenth century be explained? Take away the coal mines (the telluric environment), and you could not have the economic conditions of England as they are. For the economic conditions are a result of favorable or unfavorable telluric conditions which are acted upon by the intelligence and energy of a certain race. Catania, Messina, Syracuse, are in a better economic condition, because they have better geographical conditions and a different race (of Grecian blood) than the other Sicilian provinces. So it is in Apulia and Naples, which have likewise a considerable mixture of Grecian blood. The northern tourists are still attracted by our art and visit the ruins of Taormina or Pesto, which are the relics of the Grecian race. And it is the Grecian blood which explains the lesser frequency of bloody crimes in those provinces. This is therefore evidently the influence of the race. And I maintain that the same fact is due in the province of Benevent to the admixture of Langobardian blood. For the Duchy of Benevent has had an influx of Langobardian elements since the seventh century. And as we know that the German and Anglo-Saxon race has the smallest tendency towards bloody crimes, the beneficial influence of this racial character in Benevent explains itself. On the other hand, there is much Saracen blood in the western and southern provinces of Sicily, and this explains the greater number of bloody crimes there. It is evident that the organic character of the inhabitants of that island, where you may still see the brutal and barbarian features of the Saracen by the side of those of the blond, cool, and quiet Norman, contains a transfusion of the blood of diverse races. But it is also true that wherever a certain race has been predominant, there its influence is left behind in the individual and collective life.

Let this be enough so far as the anthropological factor of criminality is concerned. There are, furthermore, the telluric factors, that is to say, the physical environment in which we live and to which we pay no attention. It requires much philosophy, said Rousseau, to note the things with which we are in daily contact, because the habitual influence of a thing makes it more difficult to be aware of it. This applies also to the immediate influence of the physical conditions on human morality, notwithstanding the spiritualist prejudices which still weigh upon our daily lives. For instance, if it is claimed in the name of supernaturalism and psychism that a man is unhappy because he is vicious, it is equivalent to making a one-sided statement. For it is just as true to say that a man becomes vicious because he is unhappy. Want is the strongest poison for the human body and soul. It is the fountain head of all inhuman and antisocial feeling. Where want spreads out its wings, there the sentiments of love, of affection, of brotherhood, are impossible. Take a look at the figures of the peasant in the far-off arid Campagna, the little government employe, the laborer, the little shopkeeper. When work is assured, when living is certain, though poor, then want, cruel want, is in the distance, and every good sentiment can germinate and develop in the human heart. The family then lives in a favorable environment, the parents agree, the children are affectionate. And when the laborer, a bronzed statue of humanity, returns from his smoky shop and meets his white-haired mother, the embodiment of half a century of immaculate virtue and heroic sacrifices, then he can, tired, but assured of his daily bread, give room to feelings of affection, and he will cordially invite his mother to share his frugal meal. But let the same man, in the same environment, be haunted by the spectre of want and lack of employment, and you will see the moral atmosphere in his family changing as from day into night. There is no work, and the laborer comes home without any wages. The wife, who does not know how to feed the children, reproaches her husband with the suffering of his family. The man, having been turned away from the doors of ten offices, feels his dignity as an honest laborer assailed in the very bosom of his own family, because he has vainly asked society for honest employment. And the bonds of affection and union are loosened in that family. Its members no longer agree. There are too many children, and when the poor old mother approaches her son, she reads in his dark and agitated mien the lack of tenderness and feels in her mother heart that her boy, poisoned by the spectre of want, is perhaps casting evil looks at her and harboring the unfilial thought: "Better an open grave in the cemetery than one mouth more to feed at home!"

It is true that want alone is not sufficient to prepare the soil in the environment of that suffering family for the roots of real crime and to develop it. Want will weaken the love and mutual respect among the members of that family, but it will not be strong enough alone to arm the hands of the man for a matricidal deed, unless he should get into a pathological mental condition, which is very exceptional and rare. But the conclusions of the positive school are confirmed in this case as in any other. In order that crime may develop, it is necessary that anthropological, social, and telluric factors should act together.

We generally forget the conditions of the physical environment in which we live, because supernatural prejudice tells us that the body is a beast which we must forget in order to elevate ourselves into a spiritual life. Manzoni[3] could designate the Middle

3. The reference is apparently to Alessandro Manzoni, 1785–1873, Italian poet, novelist, and grandson of Cesare Beccaria.

Ages by the term "dirty," because they neglected the demands of elementary hygiene, and thus of human morality. For where the requirements of our physical body are neglected or offended, there no flower can bloom. The telluric environment has a great influence on our physical activity, by way of our nervous system. We feel differently disposed, according to whether a south or a north wind blows. When Garibaldi was on the Pampas, he observed that his companions were irascible and prone to violent quarrels when the Pampero blew, and that their behavior changed when this wind ceased. The great founders of criminal statistics, Quetelet and Guerry,[4] observed that the change of seasons carried with it a change in criminality. Sexual crimes are less frequent in winter than in spring and summer. And with reference to this point I have maintained, and still maintain, that it is due to the combined effects of temperature and social conditions, if crimes against property increase in winter. For lack of employment, the want of food and shelter, intensify the misery and lead to attacks on property. On the other hand, the cold by itself reduces sexual crimes and personal assaults. And those who claim that the longer intercourse between people in summer time has also a social influence are also partly in the right.

The most eloquent fact in this respect was mentioned by Marro,[5] when he pointed out that this change in the frequency of bloody crimes, greater in the warm months than in winter, applied also to prisoners. Statistics show that breach of discipline is most frequent in hot seasons. The social factor does not enter there, because the social life is there the same in winter and in summer. This is, therefore, a practical proof of the influence

4. André-Michel Guerry, 1802–1866, French lawyer and social statistician. For a useful discussion and comparison of the work of Quetelet and Guerry see Leon Radzinowicz, *Ideology and Crime* (New York: Columbia University Press, 1966), Ch. 2.

5. The 1906 edition contains the spelling Murro but the reference is clearly to Antonio Marro, 1840–1913, Italian doctor, prison physician, professor, student, and collaborator of Lombroso. Noted for his work with the insane and directorship of several insane asylums.

of climate, and it is re-enforced by the fact that delirium and epilepsy in insane asylums are also more frequent in hot than in cold months. The influence of the telluric factors, then, cannot be denied, and the influence of the social factor intensifies it, as I have already shown by its most drastic and characteristic example, that of want. One can, therefore, understand that a man, whose morality has been shaken by the pressure of increasing want, may be led to commit a crime against property or persons.

It is certainly quite evident that economic misery has an undeniable influence on criminality. And if you consider, that about 300,000 criminals are sentenced in Italy every year, 180,000 of them for minor crimes, and 120,000 for crimes which belong to the gravest class, you can easily see that the greater part of them are due mainly to social conditions, for which it should not be so very difficult to find a remedy. The work of the legislator may be slow, difficult, and inadequate, so far as the telluric and anthropological factors are concerned. But it could surely be rapid, efficacious, and prompt, so far as the social factors influencing criminality are concerned.

We have now demonstrated that crime has its natural source in the combined interaction of three classes of causes, the anthropological (organic and psychological) factor, the telluric factor, and the social factor. And by this last factor we must not only mean want, but any other condition of administrative instability in political, moral, and intellectual life. Every social condition which makes the life of man in society insincere and imperfect is a social factor contributing towards criminality. The economic factor is in evidence in our civilization wherever the law of free competition, which is but a form of disguised cannibalism, establishes the rule: *Your death is my life.* The competition of laborers for a limited number of places is equivalent to saying that those who secure a living do so at the expense of those who do not. And this is a disguised form of cannibalism. While it does not devour the competitor as primitive mankind did, it paralyzes him by calumnies, recommendations, protection, money, which secure the place for the best bargainer and leave the most honest, talented, and self-respecting to the pangs of starvation.

Moreover, the economic factor exerts its crime-breeding influence also under the form of a superabundance of wealth. Indeed, in our present society, which is in the downward stage of transition from glorious bourgeois civilization, which constituted a golden page of human history in the nineteenth century, wealth itself is a source of crime. For the rich, who do not enjoy the advantage of manual or intellectual work, suffer from the corruption of leisure and vice. Gambling throws them into an unhealthy fever; the struggle and race for money poison their daily lives. And although the rich may keep out of reach of the penal code, still they have condemned themselves to a life devoted to hypocritical ceremonies, which are devoid of moral sentiment. And this life leads them to a sportive form of criminality. To cheat at gambling is the inevitable fate of these parasites. In order to kill time they give themselves up to games of chance, and those who do not care for that devote themselves to the sport of adultery, which in that class is a pastime even among the best friends, on account of sheer mental poverty. And all because man's mind unoccupied is the devil's own forge, as the English poet says.

We have now surveyed briefly the natural genesis of crime as a natural social phenomenon, brought about by the interaction of anthropological, telluric, and social influences, which in any determined moment act upon a personality standing on the cross road of vice and virtue, crime and honesty. This scientific deduction gives rise to a series of investigations which satisfy the mind and supply it with a real understanding of things, far better than the theory that a man is a criminal because he wants to be. No, a man commits crime because he finds himself in certain physical and social conditions, from which the evil plant of crime takes life and strength. Thus we obtain the origin of that sad human figure which is the product of the interaction of those factors, an abnormal man, a man not adopted to the conditions of the social environment in which he is born, so that emigration becomes an ever more permanent phenomenon for the greater portion of men, for whom the accident of birth will less and less determine the course of their future life. And the abnormal man who is below the minimum of adaptability to social life and bears the marks of organic degeneration, develops either a passive or an aggressive form of abnormality and becomes a criminal.

Among these abnormal human beings, two groups must be particularly distinguished. Limiting our observations to those who are true aggressively antisocial abnormals, that is to say, who are not adapted to a certain social order and attack it by crimes, we must distinguish those who for egoistic or ferocious reasons attack society by atavistic forms of the struggle for existence by committing so-called common crimes in the shape of fraud or violence, thereby opposing or abolishing conditions in which their fellow beings may live. This is the atavistic type of criminal which represents an involutionary, or retrogressive, form of abnormality, due to an arrested development or an atavistic reversion to a savage and primitive type. These constitute the majority in the world of criminals and must be distinguished from the minority, who are evolutionary, or progressive, abnormals, that may also commit crime in a violent form, but must not be confounded with the others, because they do not act from egoistic motives, but rebel from altruistic motives against the injustice of the present order. These altruistic criminals feel the sufferings and horrors due to the injustice surrounding them and may go so far as to commit murder, which must always be condemned, but which must not be confounded with atavistic or egoistic murder. Recourse to personal violence is always objectionable from the point of view of higher manhood, which desires that human life should always be held in respect. But the reasons for such a crime are different, being egoistic in the one, and altruistic in the other case. The evolutionary abnormal is often an instrument of human progress, not in the form of criminality, but in that of intellectual and moral rebellion against

86

conditions which are sanctioned by laws that frequently punish such an evolutionary rebellion harder than atavistic crime, as they do in Russia, where capital punishment has been abolished for common crimes, but retained for political violations of the law! We are living in an epoch of transition from the old to the new, and contemporaneous humanity has an uneasy moral conscience in this critical time. The ruling classes are losing their clearness of vision, so that they promise monuments to those political murderers who promoted their own historical victories, but would condemn like any common criminal him who now devotes his soul to a revolutionary ideal, would throw into prison the pioneer of new human ideals, just as Russia is excommunicating the rebel Tolstoi. I mention Leo Tolstoi advisedly for the purpose of giving a precise illustration of my heterodox thought in reference to this question. We are opposed to any form of personal violence (with the sole exception of self-defense), we cannot approve of any form of personal assault, no matter what may be its motive. Therefore we cannot have words of praise or excuse for political murder, though it may be inspired by altruistic motives. We can demand that the legislator should distinguish between the psychological sources of these two forms of murder, the egoistic and the altruistic form. But we condemn them both, because they are inhuman forms of violence. Ideas do not make victorious headway by force of arms. Ideas must be combatted by ideas, and it is only by the propaganda of the idea that we can prepare humanity for its future. Violence is always a means of preventing the sincere and fruitful diffusion of an idea. We do not say this merely for the abnormals of the lower classes. We refer with scientific serenity also to the upper classes, who would suppress by violence every manifestation of revolt against the social iniquities, every affirmation of faith in a better future.

This is the conception of our science, which thus succeeds in distinguishing traits of character even among the unlucky and forlorn people of the criminal world, while the classic school of criminology regards a criminal as a sort of abstract and normal man, with the exception of cases of minors, deaf-mutes, inebriates, and maniacs.

In fact, the classic school of criminology regards all thieves as THE thief, all murderers as THE murderer, and the human shape disappears in the mind of the legislator, while it re-appears before the judge. Before the essayist and legislator, the criminal is a sort of moving dummy, on whose back the judge may paste an article of the penal code. If you leave out of consideration the established cases of exceptional and rare human psychology mentioned in the penal code, all other cases serve the judge merely as an excuse to select from the criminal code the number of that article which will fit the criminal dummy, and if he should paste 404 instead of 407 on its back, the court of appeals would resist any change of numbers. And if this dummy came to life and said: "The question of my number may be very important for you, but if you would study all the conditions that compelled me to take other people's things, you would realize that this importance is very diagrammatic," the judge would answer: "That's all right for the justice of the future, but it isn't now. You are number 404 of the criminal code, and after leaving this court room with this number pasted legally on your back, you will receive another number, for you will enter prison as number 404 and will exchange it for entry number 1525, or some other, because your personality as a man disappears entirely before the enactment of social justice"! And then it is pretended that this man, whose personality is thus absurdly ignored, should leave prison cured of all degeneration, and if he falls back into the path of thorns of his misery and commits another crime, the judge simply pastes another article over the other, by adding number 80 or 81, which refer to cases of relapse, to number 404!

In this way the classic school of criminology came to its unit of punishment, which it heralded as its great progress. In the Middle Ages, the diversity of punishment was greater. But in the nineteenth century the classic school of criminology combatted dishonoring punishment, corporeal punishment, confiscation, professional punishment, capital punishment, with its ideal of one sole penalty, the only panacea for crime and criminals, *prison.*

We have, indeed, prohibitory measures and fines even today. But in substance the whole punitive armory is reduced to imprisonment, since fines are likewise convertible into so many days or months of imprisonment. Solitary confinement is the ideal of the classic school of criminology. But experience proves that this penalty has as much effect on the disease of criminality as the remedy of a physician would have who would sit in the door of a hospital and tell every patient seeking relief: "Whatever may be your disease, I have only one medicine and that is a decoction of rhubarb. You have heart trouble? Well, then, the problem for me is simply—how big a dose of rhubarb decoction shall I give you?"

And measuring doses of penalty is the foundation of the criminal code. That is so true that this code is in its last analysis but a table of criminal logarithms for figuring out penalties. Woe to the judge who makes a mistake in sentencing a 19 year old offender who was drunk when he sinned, but had premeditated his deed. Woe to the judge, if he misses his calculation in adding or substracting the third, or sixth, or one half, corresponding to the prescribed extenuating or aggravating circumstances! If he makes a miscalculation, the court of appeals is invoked by the defendant, and the inexorable court of appeals tells the judge: "Figure this over again. You have been unjust." The only question for the judge is this: Add your sums and subtract your deductions, and the prisoner is sentenced to one year, seven months, and thirteen days. Not one day more or less! But the human spectator asks: "If the criminal should happen to be reformed before the expiration of his term, should he be retained in prison?" The judge replies: "I don't care; he stays in one year, seven months, and thirteen days!"

Then the human spectator says: "But suppose the criminal should not yet be fit for human society at the expiration of his term?" The judge replies: "At the expiration of his term he leaves prison, for when he has absolved his last day, he has paid his debt!"

This is the same case as that of the imaginary physician who says: "You have heart trouble? Then take a quart of rhubarb decoction and stay twelve days in the hospital." Another patient says: "I have broken my leg." And the doctor: "All right, take a pint of rhubarb decoction and 17 days in the hospital." A third has inflammation of the lungs, and the doctor prescribes three quarts of rhubarb decoction and three months in the hospital. "But if my inflammation is cured before that time?" "No matter," says the doctor, "you stay in three months." "But if I am not cured of my lung trouble after three months?" "No matter," says the doctor, "you leave after three months."

To such results have wise men been led by a system of penal justice, which is a denial of all elementary common sense. They have forgotten the personality of the criminal and occupied themselves exclusively with crime as an abstract juristic phenomenon. In the same manner, the old style medicine occupied itself with disease as such, as an abstract pathological phenomenon, without taking into account the personality of the patient. The ancient physicians did not consider whether a patient was well or ill nourished, young or old, strong or weak, nervous or fullblooded. They cured fever as fever, pleurisy as pleurisy. Modern medicine, on the other hand, declares that disease must be studied in the living person of the patient. And the same disease may require different treatment, if the condition of the patient is different.

Criminal justice has taken the same historical course of development as medicine. The classic school of criminology is still in the same stage in which medicine was before the middle of the nineteenth century. It deals with theft, murder, fraud, as such. But that which claims so much of the attention of society has been forgotten by the classic school. For that school has forgotten to study the murderer, the thief, the forger, and without that study their crimes cannot be understood.

Crime is one of the conditions required for the study of the criminal. But the same crime may require the application of different remedies to the personalities of different criminals, according to the different anthropological and social conditions of the various criminals. There is a fundamental distinction between the anthropological and social types of criminals, whom I have divided into five categories, which are today unanimously accepted by criminalist anthropologists, since the Geneva congress offered an opportunity to explain the misapprehension which led some foreign scientists to believe that the Italian school regarded one of these types (the born criminal) merely as an organic anomaly.

Just a word concerning each one of these five types.

The *born criminal* is a victim of that which I will call (seeing that science has not yet solved this problem) criminal neurosis, which is very analogous to epileptic neurosis, but which is not in itself sufficient to make one a criminal. Our adversaries had the idea that the mere possession of a crooked nose or a slanting skull stamped a man as predisposed by birth to murder or theft. But a man may be a born criminal, that is to say, he may have some congenital degeneration which predisposes him toward crime, and yet he may die at the age of 80 without having committed any crime, because he was fortunate enough to live in an environment which did not offer him any temptation to commit crime. Again, are not many predisposed toward insanity without ever becoming insane? If the same individual were to live under unfavorable conditions, without any education, if he were to find himself in unhealthy telluric surroundings, in a mine, a rice field, or a miasmatic swamp, he would become insane. But if instead of living in conditions that condemn him to lunacy he were to be under no necessity to struggle for his daily bread, if he could live in affluence, he might exhibit some eccentricity of character, but would not cross the threshold of an insane asylum. The same happens in the case of criminality. One may have a congenital predisposition toward crime, but if he lives in favorable surroundings, he will live to the end of his natural life without violating any criminal or moral law. At any rate we must drop the prejudice that only those are criminals on whose backs the judge has pasted a number. For there are many scoundrels at large who commit crime with impunity, or who brush the edge of the criminal law in the most repulsive immorality without violating it.

This misunderstanding was explained at the congress of Geneva by the statement that the interaction of the social and telluric environment is required also in the case of the born criminal. And now we may take it for granted that my classification of five types is everywhere accepted. These are the following: The *born criminal* who has a congenital predisposition for crime; the *insane criminal* suffering from some clinical form of mental alienation, and whom even our existing penal code had to recognize; the *habitual criminal*, that is to say one who has acquired the habit of crime mainly through the ineffective measures employed by society for the prevention and repression of crime. A common figure in our large industrial centers is that of the abandoned child which has to go begging from its earliest youth in order to collect an income for the enterprising boss of for [*sic*] its poor family, without an opportunity to educate its moral sense in the filth of the streets. It is punished for the first time by the law and sent to prison or to a reformatory, where it is inevitably corrupted. Then, when such an individual comes out of prison, he is stigmatized as a thief or forger, watched by the police, and if he secures work in some shop, the owner is indirectly induced to discharge him, so that he must inevitably fall back upon crime.

Thus one acquires crime as a habit, a product of social rottenness, due to the ineffective measures for the prevention and repression of crime. There is furthermore the *occasional criminal*, who commits very insignificant criminal acts, more because he is led astray by his conditions of life than because the aggressive energy of a degenerate personality impels him. If he is not made worse by a prison life, he may find an opportunity to return to a normal life in society. Finally there is the *passionate criminal*, who, like the insane criminal, has received attention from the positive school of criminology; which, however, did not come to any definite conclusions regarding him, such as may be gathered by means of the experimental method through study in prisons, insane asylums, or in freedom. The relations between passion and crime have so far been studied on a field in which no solution was possible. For the classic school considers such a crime according to the greater or smaller intensity and violence of passion and comes to the conclusion that the degree of responsibility decreases to the extent that the intensity of a passion increases, and vice versa. The problem cannot be solved in this way. There are passions which may rise to the highest degree of intensity without reducing the responsibility. For instance, is one who murders from motives of revenge a passionate criminal who must be excused?

The classic school of criminology says "No," and for my part I agree with them. Francesco Carrara says: "There are blind passions, and others which are reasonable. Blind passions deprive one of free will, reasonable ones do not. Blind and excusable passions are fear, honor, love, reasonable and inexcusable ones are hatred and revenge." But how so? I have studied murderers who killed for revenge and who told me that the desire for revenge took hold of them like a fever, so that they "forgot even to eat." Hate and revenge can take possession of a man to such an extent that he becomes blind with passion. The truth is that passion must be considered not so far as its violence or quantity are concerned, but rather as to its quality. We must distinguish between social and antisocial passion, the one favoring the conditions of life for the species and collectivity, the other antagonistic to the development of the collectivity. In the first case, we have love, injured honor, etc., which are passions normally useful to society, and aberrations of which may be excused more or less according to individual cases. On the other hand, we have inexcusable passions, because their psychological tendency is to antagonize the development of society. They are antisocial, and cannot be excused, and hate and revenge are among them.

The positive school therefore admits that a passion is excusable, when the moral sense of a man is normal, when his past record is clear, and when his crime is due to a social passion, which makes it excusable.

We shall see tomorrow what remedies the positive school of criminology proposes for each one of these categories of criminals, in distinction from the measuring of doses of imprisonment advocated by the classic school.

We have thus exhausted in a short and general review the subject of the natural origin of criminality. To sum up, crime is a social phenomenon, due to the interaction of anthropological, telluric, and social factors. This law brings about what I have called criminal saturation, which means that every society has the criminality which it deserves, and which produces by means of its geographical and social conditions such quantities and qualities of crime as correspond to the development of each collective human group.

Thus the old saying of Quetelet[6] is confirmed: "There is an annual balance of crime, which must be paid and settled with greater regularity than the accounts of the national revenue." However, we positivists give to this statement a less fatalistic interpretation, since we have demonstrated that crime is not our immutable destiny, even though it is a vain beginning to attempt to attenuate or eliminate crime by mere schemes. The truth is that the balance of crime is determined by the physical and social environment. But by changing the condition of the social environment, which is most easily modified, the legislator may alter the influence of the telluric environment and the organic and psychic conditions of the population, control the greater portion of crimes, and reduce them considerably. It is our firm conviction that a truly civilized legislator can attenuate the plague of criminality, not so much by means of the criminal code, as by means of remedies which are latent in the remainder of the social life and of legislation. And the experience of the most advanced countries confirms this by the beneficent and preventive influence of criminal legislation resting on efficacious social reforms.

We arrive, then, at this scientific conclusion: In the society of the future, the necessity for penal justice will be reduced to the extent that social justice grows intensively and extensively.

6. The spelling Imetelet appears in the 1906 edition.

LECTURE III
[REMEDIES]

IN the preceding two lectures, I have given you a short review of the new current in scientific thought, which studies the painful and dangerous phenomena of criminality. We must now draw the logical conclusions, in theory and practice, from the teachings of experimental science, for the removal of the gangrenous plague of crime. Under the influence of the positive methods of research, the old formula "Science for science's sake" has given place to the new formula "Science for life's sake." For it would be useless for the human mind to retreat into the vault of philosophical concentration, if this intellectual mastery did not produce as a counter-effect a beneficent wave of real improvement in the destinies of the human race.

What, then, has the civilized world to offer in the way of remedies against criminality? The classic school of criminology, being unable to locate in the course of its scientific and historical mission the natural causes of crime, as I have shown in the preceding lectures, was not in a position to deal in a comprehensive and far-seeing manner with this problem of the remedy against criminality. Some of the classic criminologists, such as Bentham, Romagnosi, or Ellero, with a more positive bent of mind than others, may have given a little of their scientific activity to the analysis of this problem, namely the prevention of crime. But Ellero himself had to admit that "the classic school of criminology has written volumes concerning the death penalty and torture, but has produced but a few pages on the prevention of criminality." The historical mission of that school consisted in a reduction of punishment. For being born on the eve of the French revolution in the name of individualism and natural rights, it was a protest against the barbarian penalties of the Middle Ages. And thus the practical and glorious result of the classic school was a propaganda for the abolition of the most brutal penalties of the Middle Ages, such as the death penalty, torture, mutilation. We in our turn now follow up the practical and scientific mission of the classic school of criminology with a still more noble and fruitful mission by adding to the problem of the *diminution of penalties* the problem of the *diminution of crimes*. It is worth more to humanity to reduce the number of crimes than to reduce the dread sufferings of criminal punishments, although even this is a noble work, after the evil plant of crime has been permitted to grow in the realm of life. Take, for instance, the philanthropic awakening due to the Congress of Geneva in the matter of the Red Cross Society, for the care, treatment, and cure of the wounded in war. However noble and praiseworthy this mission may be, it would be far nobler and better to prevent war than to heal the mutilated and wounded. If the same zeal and persistence, which have been expended in the work of the Red Cross Society, had been devoted to the realization of international brotherhood, the weary road of human progress would show far better results.

It is a noble mission to oppose the ferocious penalties of the Middle Ages. But it is still nobler to forestall crime. The classic school of criminology directed its attention merely to penalties, to repressive measures after crime had been committed, with all its terrible moral and material consequences. For in the classic school, the remedies against criminality have not the social aim of improving human life, but merely the illusory mission of retributive justice, meeting a moral delinquency by a corresponding punishment in the shape of legal sentences. This is the spirit which is still pervading criminal legislation, although there is a sort of eclectic compromise between the old and the new. The classic school of criminology has substituted for the old absolutist conceptions of justice the eclectic theory that absolute justice has the right to punish, but a right modified by the interests of civilized life in present society. This is the point discussed in Italy in the celebrated controversy between Pasquale Stanislao Mancini and Terencio Mamiani,[1] in 1847. This is in substance the theory followed by the classic criminologists who revised the penal code, which public opinion considers incapable of protecting society against the dangers of crime. And we have but to look about us in the realities of contemporaneous life in order to see that the criminal code is far from being a remedy against crime, that it remedies nothing, because either premeditation or passion in the person of the criminal deprive the criminal law of all prohibitory power. The deceptive faith in the efficacy of criminal law still lives in the public mind, because every normal man feels that the thought of imprisonment would stand in his way, if he contemplated tomorrow committing a theft, a rape, or a murder. He feels the bridle of the social sense. And the criminal code lends more strength to it and holds him back from criminal actions. But even if the criminal code did not exist, he would not commit a crime, so long as his physical and social environment would not urge him in that direction. The criminal code serves only to isolate

1. Terencio Mamiani, 1799–1885, Italian writer, philosopher, political theorist, and professor; noted for the series of letters exchanged with Mancini in 1841. Mamiani argued, in opposition to Mancini, that the objectives of law and morality were identical and that punishment must reward evil with evil. See Lecture I, note 21.

temporarily from social intercourse those who are not considered worthy of it. And this punishment prevents the criminal for a while from repeating his criminal deed. But it is evident that the punishment is not imposed until after the deed has been done. It is a remedy directed against effects, but it does not touch the causes, the roots, of the evil.

We may say that in social life penalties have the same relation to crime that medicine has to disease. After a disease has developed in an organism, we have recourse to a physician. But he cannot do anything else but to reach the effects in some single individual. On the other hand, if the individual and the collectivity had obeyed the rules of preventive hygiene, the disease would have been avoided 90 times in 100, and would have appeared only in extreme and exceptional cases, where a wound or an organic condition break through the laws of health. Lack of providence on the part of man, which is due to insufficient expression of the forces of the intellect and pervades so large a part of human life, is certainly to blame for the fact that mankind chooses to use belated remedies rather than to observe the laws of health, which demand a greater methodical control of one's actions and more foresight, because the remedy must be applied before the disease becomes apparent. I say occasionally that human society acts in the matter of criminality with the same lack of forethought that most people do in the matter of tooth-ache. How many individuals do not suffer from tooth-ache, especially in the great cities? And yet any one convinced of the miraculous power of hygiene could easily clean his teeth every day and prevent the microbes of tooth rot from thriving, thereby saving his teeth from harm and pain. But it is tedious to do this every day. It implies a control of one's self. It cannot be done without the scientific conviction that induces men to acquire this habit. Most people say: "Oh well, if that tooth rots, I'll bear the pain." But when the night comes in which they cannot sleep for tooth-ache, they will swear at themselves for not having taken precautions and will run to the dentist, who in most cases cannot help them any more.

The legislator should apply the rules of social hygiene in order to reach the roots of criminality. But this would require that he should bring his mind and will to bear daily on a legislative reform of individual and social life, in the field of economics and morals as well as in that of administration, politics, and intelligence. Instead of that, the legislators permit the microbes of criminality to develop their pathogenic powers in society. When crimes become manifest, the legislator knows no other remedy but imprisonment in order to punish an evil which he should have prevented. Unfortunately this scientific conviction is not yet rooted and potent in the minds of the legislators of most of the civilized countries, because they represent on an average the backward scientific convictions of one or two previous generations. The legislator who sits in parliament today was the university student of thirty years ago. With a few very rare exceptions he is supplied only with knowledge of outgrown scientific research. It is a historical law that the work of the legislator is always behind the science of his time. But nevertheless the scientist has the urgent duty to spread the conviction that hygiene is worth as much on the field of civilization as it is in medicine for the public health.

This is the fundamental conviction at which the positive school arrives: That which has happened in medicine will happen in criminology. The great value of practical hygiene, especially of social hygiene, which is greater than that of individual hygiene, has been recognized after the marvelous scientific discoveries concerning the origin and primitive causes of the most dangerous diseases. So long as Pasteur and his disciples had not given to the world their discovery of the pathogenic microbes of all infectious diseases, such as typhoid fever, cholera, diphtheria, tuberculosis, etc., more or less absurd remedies were demanded of the science of medicine. I remember, for instance, that I was compelled in my youth, during an epidemic of cholera, to stay in a closed room, in which fumigation was carried on with substances irritating the bronchial tubes and lungs without killing the cholera microbes, as was proved later on. It was not until the real causes of those infectious diseases were discovered, that efficient remedies could be employed against them. An aqueduct given to a center of population like Naples is a better protection against cholera than drugs, even after the disease has taken root in the midst of the people of Naples. This is the modern lesson which we wish to teach in the field of criminology, a field which will always retain its repressive functions as an exceptional and ultimate refuge, because we do not believe that we shall succeed in eliminating all forms of criminality. Hence, if a crime manifests itself, repression may be employed as one of the remedies of criminology, but it should be the very last, not the exclusively dominating one, as it is today.

It is this blind worship of punishment which is to blame for the spectacle which we witness in every modern country, the spectacle that the legislators neglect the rules of social hygiene and wake up with a start when some form of crime becomes acute, and that they know of no better remedy than an intensification of punishment meted out by the penal code. If one year of imprisonment is not enough, we'll make it ten years, and if an aggravation of the ordinary penalty is not enough, we'll pass a law of exception. It is always the blind trust in punishment which remains the only remedy of the public conscience and which always works to the detriment of morality and material welfare, because it does not save the society of honest people and strikes without curing those who have fallen a prey to guilt and crime.

The positive school of criminology, then, aside from the greater value attributed to daily and systematic measures of social hygiene for the prevention of criminality, comes to radically different conclusions also in the matter of repressive justice. The classic school has for a cardinal remedy against crime a preference for one kind of punishment, namely imprisonment, and gives fixed and prescribed doses of this remedy. It is the logical conclusion of retributive justice that it travels by way of an illusory purification from moral guilt to the legal responsibility of the criminal and thence on to a corresponding dose of punishment, which has been previously prescribed and fixed.

We, on the other hand, hold that even the surviving form of repression, which will be inevitable in spite of the application of the rules of social prevention, should be widely different, on account of the different conception which we have of crime and of penal justice.

In the majority of cases, composed of minor crimes committed by people belonging to the most numerous and least dangerous class of occasional or passionate criminals, the only form of civil repression will be *the compensation of the victim for his loss*. According to us, this should be the only form of penalty imposed in the majority of minor crimes committed by people who are not dangerous. In the present practice of justice the compensation of the victim for his loss has become a laughing stock, because this victim is systematically forgotten. The whole attention of the classic school has been concentrated on the juridical entity of the crime. The victim of the crime has been forgotten, although this victim deserves philanthropic sympathy more than the criminal who has done the harm. It is true, every judge adds to the sentence the formula that the criminal is responsible for the injury and the costs to another authority. But the process of law puts off this compensation to an indefinite time, and if the victim succeeds a few years after the passing of the sentence in getting any action on the matter, the criminal has in the meantime had a thousand legal subterfuges to get away with his spoils. And thus the law itself becomes the breeding ground of personal revenge, for Filangieri says aptly that an innocent man grasps the dagger of the murderer, when the sword of justice does not defend him.

Let us say at this point that the rigid application of compensation for damages should never be displaced by imprisonment, because this would be equivalent to sanctioning a real class distinction. For the rich can laugh at damages, while the proletarian would have to make good a sentence of 1000 lire by 100 days in prison, and in the meantime the innocent family that tearfully waits for him outside would be plunged into desperate straits. Compensation for damages should never take place in any other way than by means of the labor of the prisoner to an extent satisfactory to the family of the injured. It has been attempted to place this in an eclectic way on our law books, but this proposition remains a dead letter and is not applied in Italy, because a stroke of legislator's pen is not enough to change the fate of an entire nation.

These practical and efficient measures would be taken in the case of lesser criminals. For the graver crimes committed by atavistic or congenital criminals, or by persons inclining toward crime from acquired habit or mental alienation, the positive school of criminology reserves segregation for an indefinite time, for it is absurd to fix the time beforehand in the case of a dangerous degenerate who has committed a grave crime.

The question of indeterminate sentences has been recently discussed also by Pessina, who combats it, of course, because the essence of the classic school of criminology is retribution for a fault by means of corresponding punishment. We might reply that no human judge can use any other but the grossest scale by which to determine whether you are responsible to the extent of the whole, one half, or one third. And since there is no absolute or objective criterion by which the ratio of crime to punishment can be determined, penal justice becomes a game of chance. But we content ourselves by pointing out that segregation for an indefinite time has so much truth in it, that even the most orthodox of the classic school admit it, for instance in the case of criminals under age. Now, if an indeterminate sentence is a violation of the principles of the classic school, I cannot understand why it can be admitted in the case of minors, but not in the case of adults. This is evidently an expedient imposed by the exigencies of practical life, and only the positive school of criminology can meet them by a logical systematization. For the rest, indefinite segregation, such as we propose for the most dangerous atavistic criminals, is a measure which is already in use for ordinary lunatics as well as for criminal lunatics. But it may be said that this is an administrative measure, not a court sentence. Well, if any one is so fond of formulas as to make this objection, he may get all the fun out of them that he likes. But it is a fact that an insane person who has committed a crime is sent to a building with iron bars on its gates such as a prison has. You may call it an administrative building or a penal institute, the name is unessential, for the substance alone counts. We maintain that congenital or pathological criminals cannot be locked up for a definite term in any institution, but should remain there until they are adapted for the normal life of society.

This radical reform of principles carries with it a radical transformation of details. Given an indeterminate segregation, there should be organs of guardianship for persons so secluded, for instance permanent committees for the periodical revision of sentences. In the future, the criminal judge will always secure ample evidence to prove whether a defendant is really guilty, for this is the fundamental point. If it is certain that he has committed the crime, he should either be excluded from social intercourse or sentenced to make good the damage, provided the criminal is not dangerous and the crime not grave. It is absurd to sentence a man to five or six days imprisonment for some insignificant misdemeanor. You lower him in the eyes of the public, subject him to surveillance by the police, and send him to prison from whence he will go out more corrupted than he was on entering it. It is absurd to impose segregation in prison for small errors. Compensation for injuries is enough. For the segregation of the graver criminals, the management must be as scientific as it is now in insane asylums. It is absurd to place an old pensioned soldier or a hardened bureaucrat at the head of a penal institution. It is enough to visit one of those compulsory human beehives and to see how a military discipline carries a brutal hypocrisy into it. The management of such institutions must be scientific, and the care of their inmates must be scientific, since a grave crime is always a manifestation of the pathological condition of the individual. In America there are already institutions, such as the Elmira Reformatory, where the application of the methods of the positive school of criminology has been solemnly promised. The director of the institution is a psychologist, a physician.[2] When a criminal under age is brought in, he is studied from the point of view of physiology and psychology. The treatment serves to regenerate the plants who, being young, may still be straightened up. Scientific therapeutics can do little for relapsed criminals. The present repression of crime robs the prisoner of his personality and reduces him to a number, either in mass imprisonment which corrupts him completely, or in solitary confinement, which will turn him into a stupid or raving beast.

These methods are also gradually introduced in the insane asylums. I must tell you a little story to illustrate this. When I was a professor in Pisa, eight years ago, I took my students to the penitentiaries and the asylum for the criminal insane in Montelupo, as I always used to do. Dr. Algeri,[3] the director of this asylum, showed us among others a very interesting case. This was a man of about 45, whose history was shortly the following: He was a bricklayer living in one of the cities of Toscana. He had been a normal and honest man, a very good father, until one unlucky day came, in which a brick falling from a factory broke a part of his skull. He fell down unconscious, was picked up, carried to the hospital, and cured of his external injury, but lost both his physical and moral health. He became an epileptic.

And the lesion to which the loss of the normal function of his nervous system was due transformed him from the docile and even-tempered man that he had been into a quarrelsome and irritable individual, so that he was less regular in his work, less moral and honest in his family life, and was finally sentenced for a grave assault in a saloon brawl. He was condemned as a common criminal to I don't know how many years of imprisonment. But in prison, the exceptional conditions of seclusion

2. The reference is apparently to Zebulon Reed Brockway. However, Brockway was not a physician. Similarly, only very liberal use of the term psychologist would warrant this label today.

3. The spelling Algieri appears in the 1906 edition, but the reference is apparently to Dr. G. Algeri.

brought on a deterioration of his physical and moral health, his epileptic fits became more frequent, his character grew worse. The director of the prison sent him to the asylum for the insane criminals at Montelupo, which shelters criminals suspected of insanity and insane criminals.

Dr. Algeri studied the interesting case and came to the diagnosis that there was a splinter of bone in the man's brain which had not been noticed in the treatment at the hospital, and that this was the cause of the epilepsy and demoralization of the prisoner. He trepanned a portion of the skull around the old wound and actually found a bone splinter lodged in the man's brain. He removed the splinter, and put a platinum plate over the trepanned place to protect the brain. The man improved, the epileptic fits ceased, his moral condition became as normal as before, and this bricklayer (how about the free will?) was dismissed from the asylum, for he had given proofs of normal behavior for about five or six months, thanks to the wisdom of the doctor who had relieved him of the lesion which had made him epileptic and immoral. If this asylum for insane criminals had not been in existence, he would have ended in a padded cell, the same as another man whom I and my students saw a few years ago in the Ancona penitentiary. The director, an old soldier, said to me: "Professor, I shall show you a type of human beast. He is a man who passes four-fifths of the year in a padded cell." After calling six attendants, "because we must be careful," we went to the cell, and I said to that director: "Please, leave this man to me. I have little faith in the existence of human beasts. Keep the attendants at a distance." "No," replied the director, "my responsibility does not permit me to do that."

But I insisted. The cell was opened, and the man came out of it really like a wild beast with bulging eyes and distorted face. But I met him with a smile and said to him kindly: "How are you?" This change of treatment immediately changed the attitude of the man. He first had a nervous fit and then broke into tears and told me his story with the eloquence of suffering. He said that he had some days in which he was not master of himself, but he recognized that he was good whenever the attacks of temper were over. Without saying so, he thus invoked the wisdom of human psychology for better treatment. There is indeed a physician in those prisons, but he treats generally only the ordinary diseases and is not familiar with special psychological knowledge. There may be exceptions, and in that case it is a lucky coincidence. But the prison doctor has also his practice outside and hurries through his prison work. "They simulate sickness in order to get out of prison," he says. And this will be so all the more that the physicians of our time have not sufficient training in psychology to enable them to do justice to the psychology of the criminal.

You must, therefore, give a scientific management to these institutions, and you will then render humane even the treatment of those grave and dangerous criminals, whose condition cannot be met by a simple compensation of the injury they have done to others.

This is the function of repression as we look upon it, an inevitable result of the positive data regarding the natural origin of crime.

We believe, in other words, that repression will play but an unimportant role in the future. We believe that every branch of legislation will come to prefer the remedies of social hygiene to those symptomatic remedies and apply them from day to day. And thus we come to the theory of the prevention of crime. Some say: "It is better to repress than to prevent." Others say: "It is better to prevent than to repress." In order to solve this conflict we must remember that there are two widely different kinds of repression. There is the immediate, direct empirical repression, which does not investigate the cause of criminality, but waits until the crime is about to be committed. That is police prevention. There is on the other hand a social prevention which has an indirect and more remote function, which does not wait until crime is about to be committed, but locates the causes of crime in poverty, abandoned children, trampdom, etc., and seeks to prevent these conditions by remote and indirect means. In Italy, prevention is anonymous [synonymous] with arrest. That is to say, by repression is understood only police repression. Under these circumstances, it is well to take it for granted that some of the expected crimes will be carried out, for crimes are not committed at fixed periods after first informing the police. The damage done by criminality, and especially by political and social criminality, against which police repression is particularly directed, will be smaller than that done by the abuse inseparably connected with police power. In the case of atavistic criminality, prevention does not mean handcuffing of the man who is about to commit a crime, but devising such economic and educational measures in the family and administration as will eliminate the causes of crime or attentuate them, precisely because punishment is less effective than prevention.

In other words, in order to prevent crime, we must have recourse to measures which I have called "substitutes for punishment," and which prevent the development of crime, because they go to the source in order to do away with effects.

Bentham narrates that the postal service in England, in the eighteenth century, was in the hands of stage drivers, but this service was not connected with the carrying of passengers, as became the custom later. And then it was impossible to get the drivers to arrive on time, because they stopped too often at the inns. Fines were imposed, imprisonment was resorted to, yet the drivers arrived late. The penalties did not accomplish any results so long as the causes remained. Then the idea was conceived to carry passengers on the postal stages, and that stopped the drivers from being late, because whenever they made a halt, the passengers, who had an interest in arriving on time, called the drivers and did not give them much time to linger. This is an illustration of a substitute for punishment.

Another illustration. In the Middle Ages, up to the eve of our modern civilization, piracy was in vogue. Is there anything that was not tried to suppress piracy? The pirates were persecuted like wild beasts. Whenever they were caught they were condemned to the most terrible forms of death. Yet piracy continued. Then came the application of steam navigation, and piracy disappeared as by magic. And robbery and brigandage? They withstood the death penalty and extraordinary raids by soldiers. And we witness today the spectacle of a not very serious contest between the police who want to catch a brigand, Musolino;[4] and a brigand who does not wish to be caught.

Wherever the woods are not traversed by railroads or tramways, brigandage carries on its criminal trade. But wherever railroads and tramways exist, brigandage is a form of crime which disappears. You may insist on death penalties and imprisonment, but assualt and robbery will continue, because it is connected with geographical conditions. Use on the other hand the instrument of civilization, without sentencing any one, and brigandage and robbery will disappear before its light. And if human beings in large industrial centers are hearded together in tenements and slum hotels, how can a humane judge aggravate the penalties against sexual crimes? How can the sense of shame develop among people, when young and old of both sexes are crowded together in the same bed, in the same corrupted and corrupting environment, which robs the human soul of every noble spark?

I might stray pretty far, if I were to continue these illustrations of social hygiene which will be the true solution of the problem and the supreme systematic, daily humane, and bloodless remedy against the disease of criminality. However, we have not the simple faith that in the near or far future of humanity crimes can ever be wholly eradicated. Even Socialism, which looks forward to a fundamental transformation of future society on the basis of brotherhood and social justice, cannot elevate itself to the absolute and naive faith that criminality, insanity, and suicide can ever fully disappear from the earth. But it is our firm conviction that the endemic form of criminality, insanity, and suicide will disappear, and that nothing will remain of them but rare sporadic forms caused by lesion or telluric and other influences.

Since we have made the great discovery that malaria, which

4. Benedetto Musolino, 1809–1885, Italian political roustabout, founder of the "Sons of Young Italy," active on the Left, and a leader of the Calabrian Revolt.

weighs upon so many parts in Italy, is dependent for its transmission on a certain mosquito, we have acquired the control of malarial therapeutics and are enabled to protect individuals and families effectively against malaria. But aside from this function of protecting people, there must be a social prevention, and since those malarial insects can live only in swampy districts, it is necessary to bring to those unreclaimed lands the blessing of the hoe and plow, in order to remove the cause and do away with the effects. The same problem confronts us in criminology. In the society of the future we shall undertake this work of social hygiene, and thereby we shall remove the epidemic forms of criminality. And nine-tenths of the crimes will then disappear, so that nothing will remain of them but exceptional cases. There will remain, for instance, such cases as that of the bricklayer which I mentioned, because there may always be accidents, no matter what may be the form of social organization, and nervous disorders may thus appear in certain individuals. But you can see that these would be exceptional cases of criminality, which will be easily cured under the direction of science, that will be the supreme and beneficent manager of institutes for the segregation of those who will be unfit for social intercourse. The problem of criminality will thus be solved as far as possible, because the gradual transformation of society will eliminate the swamps in which the miasma of crime may form and breed.

If we wish to apply these standards to an example which today attracts the attention of all Italy to this noble city, if we desire to carry our theories into the practice of contemporaneous life, if science is to respond to the call of life, let us throw a glance at that form of endemic criminality known as the Camorra in this city, which has taken root here just as stabbing affrays have in certain centers of Turin, and the Mafia in certain centers of Sicily. In the first place, we must not be wilfully blind to facts and refuse to see that the citizens will protect themselves, if social justice does not do so. And from that to crime there is but a short step. But which is the swampy soil in which this social disease can spread and persist like leprosy in the collective organism? It is the economic poverty of the masses, which leads to intellectual and moral poverty.

You have lately had in Naples a very fortunate struggle, which seems to have overcome one of the representatives of the high Camorra. But can we believe that the courageous work of a few public writers has touched the roots of the Camorra in this city? It would be self-deception to think so. For we see that plants blossom out again, even after the most destructive hurricane has passed over them.

The healing of society is not so easy, that a collective plague may be cured by the courageous acts of one or more individuals. The process is much slower and more complicated. Nevertheless these episodes are milestones of victory in the onward march of civilization, which will paralyze the historical manifestations of social criminality. Here, then, we have a city in which some hundred thousand people rise every morning and do not know how to get a living, who have no fixed occupation, because there is not enough industrial development to reach that methodical application of labor which lifted humanity out of the prehistoric forests. Truly, the human race progresses by two uplifting energies: War and labor.

In primitive and savage society, when the human personality did not know the check of social discipline, a military discipline held the members of the tribe together. But war, while useful in primitive society, loses its usefulness more and more, because it carries within itself the cancer that paralyzes it.

While war compels collective groups to submit to the co-ordinating discipline of human activity, it also decreases the respect for human life. The soldier who kills his fellow man of a neighboring nation by a stroke of his sword will easily lose the respect for the life of members of his own social group. Then the second educational energy interferes, the energy of labor, which makes itself felt at the decisive moment of prehistoric development, when the human race passes from a pastoral, hunting, and nomadic life into an agricultural and settled life. This is the historic stage in which the collective ownership of land and instruments of production is [are] displaced by communal property, family property, and finally individual property. During these stages, humanity passes from individual and isolated labor to collective, associated, co-ordinated labor. The remains of the neolithic epoch show us the progress of the first workshops, in which our ancestors gathered and fashioned their primitive tools and arms. They give us an idea of associated and common labor, which then becomes the great uplifting energy, because, unlike war, it does not carry within itself a disdain or violation of the rights of others.

Labor is the sole perennial energy of mankind which leads to social perfection. But if you have 100,000 persons in a city like Naples who do not enjoy the certainty and discipline of employment at methodical and common labor, you need not wonder that the uncertainty of daily life, an illfed stomach, and an anemic brain, result in the atrophy of all moral sentiment, and that the evil plant of the Camorra spreads out over everything. The processes in the law courts may attract the fleeting attention of public opinion, of legislation, of government, to the disease from which this portion of the social organism is suffering, but mere repression will not accomplish anything lasting.

The teaching of science tells us plainly that in such a case of endemic criminality social remedies must be applied to social evils. Unless the remedy of social reforms accompanies the development and protection of labor; unless justice is assured to every member of the collectivity, the courage of this or that citizen is spent in vain, and the evil plant will continue to thrive in the jungle.

Taught by the masterly and inflexible logic of facts, we come to the adoption of the scientific method in criminal research and conclude that a simple and uniform remedy like punishment is not adequate to cure such a natural and social phenomenon as crime, which has its own natural and social causes. The measures for the preservation of society against criminality must be manifold, complex and varied, and must be the outcome of persevering and systematic work on the part of legislators and citizens on the solid foundation of a systematic collective economy.

Let me take leave of you with this practical conclusion, and give my heart freedom to send to my brain a wave of fervent blood, which shall express my enduring gratitude for the reception which you have given me. Old in years, but young in spirit and energetic aspiration to every high ideal, I tender you my sincere thanks. As a man and a citizen, I thank you, because these three lectures have been for me a fountain of youth, of faith, of enthusiasm. Thanks to them I return to the other fields of my daily occupation with a greater faith in the future of my country and of humanity. To you, young Italy, I address these words of thanks, glad and honored, if my words have aroused in your soul one breath which will make you stronger and more confident in the future of civilization and social justice.

INDEX

113

Elmira Reformatory, 104
Expert, 8
Extenuating circumstances, 59–60
Facchinei, A., 51
Fascism, 31
Fahr, S., 9
Ferri, E.: anthropological research, 25–26; congresses of anthropology, 30; criminal classification, 22–24; *Criminal Sociology*, 25, 32; early life, 13, 15; editorship, 29, 30; education, 15, 16, 17, 18; English publications, 30; family, 29; fascism, 32; founds journal, 30; government service, 22; ideals of, 43–44; illusions, 64–67; Italian Parliament, 27–28, 29; labor cooperatives, 28; lawsuits, 29; late life, 38, 39; lawyer, 27, 33; legal reformer, 33–34; and Lombroso, 2–3, 17, 18, 19, 20, 24, 26; major contributions, 14; marriage, 28; Marxist, 28; orator, 24–25; in Paris, 18, 19, 20; Rocco Project, 31–32; socialism, 27–28, 31, 32; South American lectures, 30; theoretical viewpoint, 3–4; university service, 20, 24, 25, 27, 28, 29, 30; view of Positive School, 35; work pattern, 33
Filangieri, G., 48, 101
Fioretti, J., 18
Franchi, B., 15, 29
Free will, 55, 56, 57, 60; illusion of, 16, 54, 61, 62–63
Galilei, G., 19, 64, 65, 66
Galileo. *See* Galilei
Garibaldi, G., 83
Garofalo, R., 17, 18, 50
Geis, G., 2
Gibson, V., 30
Gioberti, V., 47
Goring, C., 30
Guarnieri, C., 28
Guerry, A., 3, 18, 83
Habitual criminal, 92
Haeckel, E., 65–66
Hall, J., 5, 7, 8, 9

Heinroth, J., 52–53
Howard, J., 67–68
Impallomeni, G., 29
Imprisonment, 100
Indeterminate sentence, 7, 37–38, 102–03
Individualization, 37
Insane criminal, 92
Insanity, 52–53
Involuntary crime, 56–57
Jeffery, C., 4, 5
Jury, 20
Justice, 58–59, 67
Laboulaye, E., 18
Labriola, T., 17
Legal responsibility, 27
Levin, Y., 2–3
Lindesmith, A., 2–3
Lombroso, C., 2–3, 17, 18, 19, 20, 22, 24, 26, 49–50, 77
Loria, A., 16
Luther, M., 63
Maestro, M., 51
Mafia, 109
Mamiani, T., 97
Mancini, P., 68, 97
Mannheim, H., 3, 4
Manzoni, A., 82–83
Marro, A., 83
Marxism, 28, 80
Matza, D., 3, 6
Minor criminals: treatment of, 101
Moral guilt, 54–55
Moral responsibility, 36
Morrison, W., 25
Mortara, L., 31
Musolino, B., 108
Mussolini, B., 30
New science: development of, 44–45
Occasional criminal, 92
Pagano, F., 56
Passionate criminal, 92
Pasteur, L., 99
Penal substitutes, 20
Penta, P., 49
Pessina, E., 46–47, 49, 50, 102
Pinel, P., 52, 53

Police: prevention, 106–07
Positive criminology: need for, 47, 49; birth of, 49, 55; development of, 45–46, 54–55, 60
Positive School: origin, 2–3
Positive science, 44
Prevention: merits of, 97–112; social, 106; police, 106–07
Prison systems, 27, 68
Professionalization, 31
Punishment: scale of, 48; by Classical School, 88–90
Quatrefages, J., 18, 19
Quetelet, L., 3, 18, 83, 94
Racial character, 78–80. See Cause; Anthropology
Radzinowicz, L., 2, 9
Rehabilitation, 3, 4, 8, 9, 10, 11
Repression: function of, 106
Responsibility, 56, 57–58
Retribution, 7–8, 97, 100, 101; limitation of, 100
Romagnosi, G., 75, 96
Rousseau, J., 81
Santoro, A., 24
Schafer, S., 11

Science of criminology: need for, 44–45
Scientific ideal, 6–7; development of, 64–67; faith in, 6, 67. See Science of criminology
Segregation of criminals, 103–04
Sellin, T., 3, 5
Shils, F., 11–12
Social hygiene, 10, 98, 99, 100, 106, 108–09, 111–12. See Substitutes for punishment
Socialism, 28, 31, 108
Solitary confinement, 68
Substitutes for punishment, 107. See Social hygiene
Tappan, P., 5
Tissot, A., 47
Tolstoi, L., 87
Torture, 52
Tuke, D., 52
Turati, F., 17, 18
Voluntary crime, 56–57
Wigmore, J., 31
Wolfgang, M., 3
Zanardelli, G., 22
Zimmern, H., 26
Zuccarelli, A., 49